My Guy

BARBARO

My Guy
BARBARO

A Jockey's Journey through Love, Triumph, and Heartbreak with America's Favorite Horse

EDGAR PRADO

with John Eisenberg

HARPER

An Imprint of HarperCollins*Publishers*
www.harpercollins.com

To Liliana and the kids,
and in memory of my mother, Zenaida,
and also in memory of Barbaro

Designed by Renato Stanisic

Library of Congress Cataloging-in-Publication Data is available upon request.

ISBN: 978-0-06-146418-8

08   09   10   11   12   ID/RRD   10 9 8 7 6 5 4

Contents

CONTENTS

One spring afternoon in 2007, I was sitting in the jockeys' room at Belmont Park when my cell phone buzzed, signaling the arrival of a text message. I pulled out my phone to see who was contacting me.

The message—written anonymously, in Spanish—sent a chill up my spine.

"You don't know me and I don't know you," it read, "but God put you on this earth for one purpose. Whatever you do in life, make sure you fulfill that purpose."

I was stunned.

Ramon Dominguez, my friend and fellow jockey, was sitting at the next locker. We had a race in a couple of minutes. I leaned over and showed him the message. He laughed.

"Whoever wrote that probably sent it to the wrong person," he said.

I didn't think so.

It had been almost a year since an amazing three-year-old colt named Barbaro had taken me to the highest and lowest moments of my career within a span of weeks, making me a main character in one of the most dramatic sports stories ever—one that made worldwide news, affected millions of people, and changed the horse racing industry forever. I probably touched more people as Barbaro's jockey than I had with all of my other mounts combined, and coming from a jockey who has ridden in more than 25,000 races since 1983, that's saying something.

Since my time on Barbaro, I had received thousands of letters, cards, phone calls, e-mails, and text messages from around the world. I had thought they would surely slow down and stop at some point, but it had been a year, and they were still coming. I couldn't get through a day without more people either writing, calling, or e-mailing me about Barbaro, asking me to pose for a picture because I had ridden him, or just thanking me for having been involved with him.

It was enough to make me wonder: Was my purpose in life, in fact, to have ridden that horse?

Ordinarily, I would never think that way. Racing fans get philosophical and sentimental about various horses and different aspects of the sport, but when you're on the inside, it's a grueling, cutthroat business and there's no room for sentiment or philosophy. I ride eleven and a half months a year, five or six days a week, five to seven races a day, mostly in New York and Florida, with occasional trips cross-country and around the world for important national and international races. I love the job, but it isn't an afternoon's entertainment for me, as it is for the fans; it is how I put food on the table. Every time I get on a horse, the other jockeys are trying to beat my brains in, and I'm doing my best to get past them. I learned early that you'll be sorry if you dwell for long on anything other than your next race and your next horse.

I had always thought that my purpose in life, aside from being a good husband and father, was to honor the athletic gifts God gave me and be the best jockey I could. Even though my experience with Barbaro shook me to my soul, I had continued to ride and win. But here it was, a whole year after Barbaro won the Kentucky Derby, and I was still seeing tears in people's eyes when they approached. I was still receiving emotional cards and letters, and text messages that seemed to have come from a higher place.

Because of my journey with Barbaro, I had touched people in some meaningful way. To them, I would always be the jockey of the doomed superstar the world fell in love with. It didn't matter that I had won more than 5,500 races, including the Belmont Stakes twice, on horses other than Barbaro. It wouldn't matter if I went out and won racing's Triple Crown on another horse.

Maybe that text message was right. Maybe, indeed, I had been put on this earth to take Barbaro's journey with him, share in his highs and lows, and represent to people whatever they wanted to see in me as a result. If so, I just hoped I had fulfilled my purpose.

Being religious myself, I had spoken to God about it. Barbaro's rise and fall left so many questions unanswered. Why tease us with such a wonderful athlete, only to yank him away at the peak of his glory? Why have him come so close to beating the odds stacked against him and then fall short?

A year after his greatest triumph, I think I knew some of

the answers. With millions of charitable dollars being raised in Barbaro's name, and with the public more aware now than ever of how important it is to treat racehorses with respect, I think the purpose of Barbaro's amazing talent was to attract attention and raise public awareness. He did that beautifully. And he meant so much to so many people.

In the end, it was just destiny, that's all, God's plan for that horse—a journey of such incredible talent, passion, strength, and endurance that no one would believe it if they hadn't seen it themselves.

I lived it, and I'm so happy and grateful I did. But I'll never be the same. I realize that now. I have gone on with my life and back to my place in an intensely competitive sport, but I'll never feel entirely whole again.

A little piece of me is gone.

CHAPTER 1

"What a Beautiful Racehorse . . ."

The first time I laid eyes on Barbaro, I finished what seemed like half a mile behind him in the Laurel Futurity, a race for two-year-old thoroughbreds at Laurel Park in Maryland. The date was November 19, 2005, the weather sunny and warm. I was riding another horse, a colt named Creve Coeur. Barbaro had raced just once before and was still so unknown that the track announcer called him bar-BEAR-o. But boy, he was already a rocket. He finished so far ahead of Creve Coeur and the rest of the field that I didn't see much of him other than his rear getting smaller and smaller as he disappeared into the distance.

Almost 11,000 fans were watching in the stands, mostly drawn to the track by the day's featured race, a highly rated short "sprint" event that had brought speedy horses and top jockeys to Maryland from around the country. The Futurity was part of the undercard, the slate of races leading up to the sprint. It was a turf race, run on Laurel's luscious grass course, and it had an impressive history, having been won by superstars such as Secretariat and Affirmed when they were youngsters on the rise back in the 1970s. But no horse of that caliber had won the event in years, so no one expected to see a phenomenal performance. Many of the other twelve horses in the field with Barbaro hadn't raced much and still weren't sure what they were doing.

I had heard a little, very little, about Barbaro before the race. I'm always talking to other people in racing—jockeys and their agents, horse owners and trainers, grooms and exercise riders—to stay on top of which horses are running well, where they're running, and whether I might be able to ride them. I vaguely recalled someone somewhere saying that a two-year-old colt trained by Michael Matz had run extremely well in his first race at Delaware Park, a racetrack in Wilmington, Delaware, in early October. But if the horse's name was mentioned, I didn't remember it, and the news pretty much went in one ear and out the other.

It came back to me when I looked around the paddock at Laurel as the horses in the Futurity were being saddled before the race. Barbaro looked like a man among boys. A brown bay with a splash of white between his eyes, he was a towering 17 hands tall—almost six feet—and bulged with muscles through his chest and front shoulders. Most of the other horses in the race were up to a foot shorter and noticeably thinner; they were typical equine teenagers, all legs and painfully gawky. Barbaro was the same age but, with sturdy legs, a broad rear, and a bodybuilder's physique, naturally built to run hard. He wasn't a sleek and slender classic beauty.

He was all jock, a toned heavyweight boxer just realizing how hard he could punch.

"My goodness, what a beautiful racehorse," I thought as I watched him from across the paddock.

My admiration only increased when we went out for the post parade, the eight-minute on-track warm-up that takes place before every race. This being my first time on Creve Coeur, I wanted to learn as much as I could about him before the race. Did he follow instructions? Were there moves he didn't like to make? Was he confident or nervous? Such knowledge can make all the difference in a race. I took Creve Coeur on a test drive—asked him to jog, veer to the left, veer to the right, stop suddenly. But while I focused on Creve Coeur, I couldn't help noticing Barbaro. He walked and jogged with a swagger, oozing confidence. Some handsome horses don't have a mind for racing, but he obviously did. Every horse is led through the post parade and up to the starting gate by another horse, a "lead pony," and nervous horses break out sweating before a race or lean against their pony for support because they're afraid. You can tell they would rather be anywhere else. Barbaro, clearly, was right where he wanted to be. His every move shouted, "I'm going to kick your butts!"

My friend Jose Caraballo, a Puerto Rican–born jockey who rides in Maryland and Delaware, was on him. Caraballo had also ridden him when he won his first race at Delaware Park by seven lengths a month earlier. That race had also been run on grass, as opposed to dirt, so I wasn't surprised to see Barbaro as one of the favorites in the Futurity at 3–1 odds. He had a track record, however brief. Several other horses, including a colt named Diabolical, also were being solidly backed, and Creve Coeur, a winner in his previous race, would leave the starting gate at 10–1. But Barbaro stood apart from them all.

At the end of the post parade he went into the starting gate like an experienced pro, unafraid of the tight quarters. When the gate opened and the horses burst out together, Barbaro quickly picked up speed, exhibiting impressive agility for a horse so large. Caraballo moved him up, settling him just behind and to the outside of the hard-charging early leader, a 45–1 shot named Capo dei Capi. I made a similar move on Creve Coeur and ended up two lengths behind Barbaro, off his inside shoulder.

The race was 1¹/₁₆ miles long, around two turns. We held our positions around the first turn and all the way up the backstretch, a period lasting about forty seconds, and then, as we approached the second turn, Diabolical passed to the inside of me and went for the lead. From where I sat, just behind the frontrunners, I had a perfect view of what happened next.

Capo dei Capi, as expected, reached his limit and slowed down. Caraballo maneuvered Barbaro around him and into the lead, but Barbaro clearly sensed Diabolical creeping up. The big horse accepted the challenge like a hungry bear at feeding time. Caraballo didn't whip him or hit him with the harder stick handle, and didn't even wave the stick in front of him—all tactics a jockey uses to get a horse to run faster. Caraballo just puckered his lips and made a smooching sound. That told Barbaro it was time to go. And did he ever.

The colt lowered his head, picked up speed, and, suddenly, was gone. He practically flew away from Diabolical, legs churning into a blur, breath blowing out in rhythmic, guttural exhalations. He surged to a two-length lead as he straightened into the home stretch, and then doubled that margin in the first hundred yards of the final run to the finish line. The big boy was flying!

Caraballo never flinched, but Barbaro kept charging at top speed, running with abandon, as if he were in a neck-and-neck duel down the stretch. The competition fell away. Barbaro was eight lengths ahead of second-place Diabolical when he crossed under the wire that stretches across the finish line. The rest of us needed binoculars to see him. Creve Coeur ended up almost twenty lengths back, having lost eighteen lengths in the last quarter mile. My horse had basically stopped running when he saw Barbaro pull away. I swore the sight had depressed him.

But it thrilled me.

When you see a horse accelerate and finish like that, especially a two-year-old just starting to race, you know you're seeing something special. Barbaro reminded me of Kitten's Joy, a champion turf horse I had ridden the year before. He was, like Barbaro, a cool customer during the post parade, and like Barbaro, he floated across the grass early in a race. But when it was time to run, he accelerated with such force that you felt the pressure in your chest.

Both horses resembled sports cars more than animals when they picked up speed, and Barbaro, at two, was only half as old as Kitten's Joy, so there was no telling how fast he might eventually go. The prospect sent a charge through me. I like speed. I've got a touch of the daredevil in me. When I'm on the highway and a Lamborghini shoots by me at 90 mph, my first thought is, I wonder what it feels like to drive that baby?

Watching Barbaro finish the Laurel Futurity, I wondered what it felt like to ride him.

After the race I said to Caraballo, "Wow, Jose, that's a nice horse—a very nice horse."

Caraballo smiled and shook his head from side to side. "And he did all that by himself. I never touched him," Jose said.

That night I flew back to New York, where I live and ride most of the year. My agent, Bob Frieze, who helps me decide which horses to ride, had booked me on horses in six races the next day at the Aqueduct race course—a typical workday for me. When Bob and I spoke on the phone to go over my schedule, as we do every day, he asked about my trip to Maryland. I told him about the Futurity and said I would love to ride Barbaro if Michael Matz ever wanted to change jockeys.

I wasn't trying to steal the ride, or "mount" as we say in the business, from Caraballo. It was just that Matz raced mostly at mid-Atlantic tracks—his barn was at the Fair Hill Training Center, near the Maryland-Delaware line—but he occasionally took his better horses to New York, or even to Florida, where I also have a home and race from January to early April. I thought Matz might take Barbaro to Florida that winter to test him against tougher competition, and might be looking for a new rider if so.

Bob said he would call Michael and express my interest.

Michael had become a trainer after a long career as a show jumper, maneuvering powerful horses over high fences; he had earned six national titles and an Olympic silver medal, and like many people with that kind of background, he really cared about his horses' well-being. He didn't push them beyond their limits in training. He kept them at Fair Hill, a peaceful, wooded park, rather than at a noisy track. He didn't have a huge stable, but I had ridden several of his better horses and they came to the races happy and ready to run.

Michael and I had always been friendly, but I hadn't ridden a horse for him in over a year because he and my agent were feuding. They had gotten into a spat over a horse Michael trained named Kicken Kris. I won a race on him at Belmont in June 2004, convincing Michael to run him in the Arlington Million, a big summertime race in Chicago. I thought it was a lock that I would ride him there, but Bob had already booked me on another horse in the race. When the trainer of that horse backed out, I committed to Kicken Kris, but the trainer then changed his mind again a few days before the race and decided to run. That meant we had committed to two horses, and Bob said I should ride the other one. Michael was furious. No trainer wants to have to look for a jockey five days before a million-dollar race.

As it turned out, Michael located a good jockey, Kent Desormeaux, and Kicken Kris won the Arlington Million while I finished second. But Michael continued to hold a grudge. I saw him later that summer and asked if we were still friends. He said yes, we were, but he would no longer use me as long as Bob was my agent. He stuck to his word for the rest of 2004 and well into 2005. We were cordial, but he didn't budge.

Finally, there was a thaw. Michael still refused to deal with Bob but called me a few times asking if I could ride several of his horses. I couldn't because of prior commitments but told him to keep me in mind. Now that Barbaro was in the picture, I thought it was time for us to get back together.

Meanwhile, a week after the Laurel Futurity I flew to Japan to compete in the World Racing Championships, an international event that draws horses and jockeys from across Asia, Europe, and the Americas. Michael refused to take Bob's call, but he called my cell phone while I was in Japan. Sitting in my hotel room after a long day at the track, I told him I was very impressed with Barbaro and would love to get on him if the opportunity ever arose. Michael listened and said we would speak after I got back from Japan.

As I learned later, Michael then called Roy and Gretchen Jackson, Barbaro's owners. I had known them since the 1990s when I was riding in Maryland and had raced a few of their horses. Barbaro's mother, La Ville Rouge, was one of the horses I had ridden for them. I didn't know them well, but I knew they lived on a farm in Pennsylvania, loved their horses, and were always friendly and appreciative of my efforts, win or lose. Roy, whose mother was a Rockefeller, was reserved, always well dressed, and looked younger than his age, which was close to seventy. Earlier in his life he had been a minor-league baseball executive and owned a sports agency. Gretchen was slender and sharp, wore large, circular wire-rimmed glasses, and was endlessly enthusiastic about her horses.

They had bred Barbaro themselves, I learned later, matching La Ville Rouge with Dynaformer, a horse that had become a much-desired stallion after a decent racing career. Dynaformer had won just seven of thirty races himself, but the sons and daughters he began fathering in 1990 had won at a much higher rate. Originally, the owners of mares had paid $5,000 for a breeding session with him, but by the time the Jacksons brought La Ville Rouge to him at Three Chimneys Farm in Midway, Kentucky, in the spring of 2002, the price for a romp was $50,000.

The Jacksons had bred horses for years, and had recently asked an expert to study their fifteen mares and suggest possible matches that might produce a winner. They wound up matching La Ville Rouge with Dynaformer, in part because she was on the small side, less than 16 hands tall, and Dynaformer was big.

The Jacksons lived on a beautiful farm in West Grove, Pennsylvania, but they kept La Ville Rouge at Sanborn Chase Farm, in Nicholasville, Kentucky, during her pregnancy. She delivered her foal by Dynaformer on April 29, 2003. He was one of a pack of babies that roamed Sanborn Chase's fields that year, and the staff noticed that he was a natural leader, big and fast, and liked to run. At one point he developed a splint—a bony deposit that swelled up—in one front leg and had to stay in his stall for two weeks, but otherwise he was perfectly healthy. The Jacksons visited him several times and named him after one of the six foxhounds identified in an oil painting hanging in their living room.

Barbaro left Kentucky in the fall of 2004 and went to a

thoroughbred training facility near Ocala, Florida, to learn to become a racehorse. He was broken—taught to accept having a rider on his back—and introduced to the starting gate. His serious training began when he was shipped from Florida to Fair Hill in the spring of 2005 to become one of Michael's students.

Michael put him on a typical training schedule consisting of daily morning gallops with an occasional "work," or harder sprint, mixed in. Michael was impressed with his size and speed. So was Michael's assistant trainer and chief exercise rider, Peter Brette. An accomplished ex-jockey from England who had raced at the highest levels in Britain and Dubai, Peter got on Barbaro every morning and was amazed by his athleticism and acceleration. The young horse was a dream to ride.

By the fall, Barbaro was ready, Michael thought, so he was entered in a "maiden" event (for nonwinners and first-timers) at Delaware Park. No one saw him coming. He went off as a 10–1 shot. That would never happen again.

Maiden races can be wild affairs, with young horses veering off in different directions, but Barbaro knew what he was doing. Caraballo placed him second early on and turned him loose rounding the turn, just like in the Laurel Futurity. Barbaro ran away from everyone.

"This could be a good one!" the Delaware Park track announcer exclaimed as Barbaro crossed the finish line.

His Laurel Futurity victory six weeks later made it two runaways in two starts, and as I suspected, Michael and the

Jacksons decided to send him to Florida for the winter racing season to test him against better horses.

After my call, Michael, Peter, and the Jacksons had several conversations about who should ride the horse in Florida. A number of the top New York–based jockeys, like me, were headed south for the winter and would be available. Caraballo had ridden the horse perfectly, but Michael and Peter discussed it, and Michael knew he would be criticized by fans and handicappers if Barbaro were beaten without having a top jockey.

"These jockeys are down here where the horse is, and Jose is up there," Michael told the Jacksons from Florida in early December. "If you want Jose, I'm sure Jose would love to come down and ride him. He hasn't done one thing wrong with the horse. But you have all these good riders here, and if you can get one to stick with Barbaro all winter, that would be the best situation. Edgar has expressed interest."

The Jacksons told Michael they were happy to have me ride Barbaro. When Michael and I spoke after my trip to Japan, he outlined the tentative conditions of an agreement. He said he would deal only with me, not Bob; he would tell me where and when Barbaro raced, and expect me to be there. As well, he wanted my word that I would be there in case a conflict arose like the one that had gotten us in trouble before.

"Look, Michael," I told him, "wherever that horse runs, I will ride him. I will be there."

Before we agreed to a deal, I called Bob to run all this by him. Bob told me he wanted to commit to various horses in the coming months—that was his job, to get me on as many good horses as possible. I told him all that was fine, but I was committing to Barbaro and giving Michael my word, so this horse would always come first. Bob said that was fine.

I called Michael and told him I would ride Barbaro, no questions asked. Michael said we had a deal.

I smiled as I hung up. I was being handed the keys to a Lamborghini.

CHAPTER 2

Shakespeare, Picasso, Barbaro

Although I'm based in New York and Florida, I regularly fly to California, Kentucky, Maryland, and elsewhere to ride in important races, and also travel three or four times a year to Peru, my native country, to see family. Airplane travel is part of my job. I fly tens of thousands of miles a year, so much that I sometimes feel like I'm on planes more than horses.

But even for a frequent flyer like me, my schedule at the end of 2005 was extreme. After the World Racing Championships in Japan, I flew to Hong Kong and rode there for several days, then flew seventeen hours home to New York, showered, changed, and went right back to the airport for a flight to my hometown, Lima, Peru. My seventy-six-year-old mother, Zenaida, was fighting breast cancer, and I was doing my best to see her as often as possible.

After spending several days with her in Lima, I flew back to Florida, picked up my family and flew to Saratoga, New

York, for a Christmas vacation. My daughter, Patty, who was twelve, and my youngest son, Louis, eleven, had said they wanted to play in the snow, so my wife Liliana and I took them north for the holidays with our older son, Edgar Jr., who was nineteen.

But as I went here, there, and everywhere, I always knew where I would be as soon as 2006 began—in Miami, at Calder Race Course, riding Barbaro for the first time in the Tropical Park Derby on New Year's Day. That was the spot Michael had selected to debut the horse in Florida—a 1¹/8-mile race on grass—and I viewed it as a statement of his long-term intentions. Barbaro, it appeared, would be a turf specialist, running in grass events rather than on dirt.

Dirt racing dominates in the United States, unlike in England and Europe, where almost all racing is conducted on turf. But most major American tracks have turf courses, and there are many high-profile turf events, including several in the Breeders' Cup, a series of multimillion-dollar races run every fall. Barbaro wouldn't compete in the Kentucky Derby, Preakness Stakes, and Belmont Stakes—the springtime Triple Crown series for three-year-olds—if he raced on the turf, but he could still have a huge career competing in turf events such as the Arlington Million, Virginia Derby, and Breeders' Cup Turf.

I liked the idea of racing Barbaro on turf. I had a lot of experience on the surface. I had won a lot of turf races at the Hipódromo de Monterrico, the racetrack in Lima where I first rode as a teenager in the early 1980s before I came to the United States. My first big stakes win in America was in a turf race, the 1991 Budweiser International at Laurel. My riding style was a good fit for the turf. Turf races are generally slower-paced and end with wild dashes to the finish, so a jockey needs to have patience and outmaneuver rivals at the end. I like to race along the inner rail, behind the early leaders, waiting for holes to open in front of me in the stretch. Then I accelerate at the right moment. I have won thousands of races on dirt that way, but the style really works on the turf.

Although horses occasionally are switched from one surface to the other, most stick to one throughout their careers. I agreed with Michael and thought it made sense to keep Barbaro on the turf. He had run away from all of his competitors in his first two starts, so he obviously loved the surface. Why change what was working? Also, his pedigree screamed turf. Dynaformer had set a track record in a turf race years earlier, and had sired many winning turf horses. Barbaro, quite simply, had the looks and makings of a classic turf horse. When I approached Michael about riding him, I hadn't expected to compete in the Triple Crown on him.

Across the country from January to late April, some three dozen stakes events for three-year-olds make up what is known as the Kentucky Derby prep season: races such as the Florida Derby, Blue Grass Stakes in Kentucky, Santa Anita Derby in California, and Wood Memorial in New York, all designed to narrow the field of Derby contenders and get the best ones in shape for the race on the first Saturday in May. Those prep races are all run on dirt, like the Derby itself. The Tropical Park Derby is run on grass.

I flew from Saratoga back to Miami a few days before the race so, after all my traveling and a little time off, I could get adjusted and prepare to compete again. Liliana, Patty, and Louis live in Florida most of the year because the kids go to school there, so I awoke on New Year's Day in our house just north of Miami. As I often do on days when I ride in the afternoon, I went to the gym at 8:00 a.m. and ran a couple of miles on a treadmill wearing a long-sleeved plastic suit, hoping to sweat off a few pounds. I weigh 115 pounds and don't have to struggle *too* hard to stay at that weight, but it does take effort and discipline. I exercise every day and eat almost nothing until dinner, just a banana or toast for breakfast and maybe an energy bar or slice of turkey meat for lunch. Dinner then needs to be well balanced, with no dessert. There isn't any room for error. Jockeys are weighed before and after each race, and if you're over the limit, which varies from race to race, you can't ride.

Before the Tropical Park Derby I ate a banana, drank a cup of coffee, drove to the track late in the morning, and set up shop in the jockeys' room, the locker room in which the riders hang out during the day. Every track has one. I have a locker for my clothes, saddles, and other riding equipment, and an assistant, called a valet, helps me get through the day. After every race I shower and change into the silks, or uniform, of the horse I'm riding in the next race. The valet makes sure everything is cleaned and ready as the day goes on, and also brings me Gatorade and juice to keep me hydrated.

The jockeys' room usually includes a kitchen and lunch counter, and a lounge with a TV and pool table. It's an interesting place. Jockeys are intensely competitive athletes, and our livelihoods depend on beating each other; nine times a day we leave the starting gate together and proceed to cut each other off, throw elbows, and curse like sailors. But when the race is over, we go back to the same locker room, share a valet, watch replays together, and debate what happened. Then we go out and do it again.

Could the New York Yankees and Boston Red Sox live together like that? No way! But we do.

Inevitably, there are angry words and bad feelings, and sometimes guys have to step outside and settle their differences. But we're also a band of brothers, the only people who know what it's like to try to steer a thousand-pound animal going 35 mph. Some of my best friends are the people I try desperately to beat. We laugh during the day, breaking the tension with jokes. And when one of us is injured, the others rush in to support him (or her) as if they're family. Which, in a sense, they are.

On the afternoon of the Tropical Park Derby, I rode in several of the early races and hung out in the jockeys' room, thinking about Barbaro. On the turf, a jockey needs to consider the condition of the course as well as his horse's running style. For instance, the turf course at Keeneland Race Course, in Lexington, Kentucky, is slow in the spring because Kentucky gets a lot of rain then, so you have to make your finishing move sooner to make sure the horse has enough time to get up to speed. The turf course at New York's Saratoga Race Course is dry and fast in the summer, so you can wait and move later. Calder's turf course was even faster, especially in

January after months of nonstop racing; it was ground down, almost a dirt course. I figured Barbaro would be able to accelerate and reach top speed in a hurry, so I could hold off making a move until very late in the game.

When it was finally time for the race, my valet handed me the green-and-blue silks of the Jacksons' Lael Stable. I put on the shirt and went down to the paddock to get on the horse. I hadn't seen Barbaro since the Laurel Futurity. He was even larger and more fearsome-looking than I recalled, and antsy at first, trying to bite his groom, a quiet Spanish-speaking guy named Jose. When I tried to pet the horse, he tried to bite me, too. He was excited. He wanted to run.

The Jacksons were there along with Michael and Peter Brette. I had never met Peter, and he sought me out before I got on the horse. He told me not to fear putting Barbaro near the front in the early going because the horse broke well from the starting gate and had what trainers call "tactical speed," meaning he could run fast early but still save a burst for the stretch. Mainly Peter told me to ride Barbaro with confidence because, he said, the horse excelled in every way. Some trainers and assistants tell you that, and it turns out that confidence isn't justified. Believe me, plenty of people say their horse is training well when it isn't. I have learned to be skeptical. When Peter told me about Barbaro, I thought, "OK, let's see if he is right."

He was.

Barbaro stopped trying to bite everyone when Michael put the saddle on him. As young as he was, he knew it was time to go to work.

I looked him in the eye before I got on him, and he gave me a level gaze in return, which was encouraging. Some horses are too hyper to hold a gaze before a race. Barbaro was cool. It was as if he was telling me, "Come on, let's go do it."

In the post parade I went through my routine—asked him to jog, stop, veer both ways, tuck behind the pony. He passed every test. There was, it seemed, no move he was afraid to do. And he wasn't nervously studying the competition, as some horses do when they lack confidence. An unsure horse stares at his rivals before a race, as if to say, "I'm not sure I can do this." Barbaro paid little attention to the other horses.

Even before we went into the starting gate—before we took one step together in competition—I was thinking how much I liked him.

The Tropical Park Derby had a dozen entrants. Barbaro was the 2–5 favorite, mainly because of his Laurel race. He went into the starting gate without a fight and stood calmly until the gate opened, and then he came out running hard, as advertised. I rode him like a favorite, positioning him near the front, in second place, a couple of lengths behind the frontrunner, a sprinter named Mr. Silver. The next horse was a few lengths back, so Barbaro could spread out and relax into his stride.

His running style was, to me, a work of art. Other people admire books by Shakespeare, paintings by Picasso, or touchdown passes by Peyton Manning. I love a great grass horse. They attack a track differently than dirt horses. They center themselves lower, almost in a squat, and glide across the grass, reaching out with their front legs as if they're long jumpers trying to see how far they can go, instead of reaching down, as dirt horses do, to dig through the dirt.

Barbaro's action was so smooth, it almost seemed he was ice-skating. I had ridden a lot of grass horses, but had never experienced such a pronounced gliding sensation.

I kept him in second around the first turn and all the way up the backside, in no hurry to take a run at the lead. In front of us, Mr. Silver surged ahead by three lengths.

As we angled into the turn, Barbaro began to move on his own and crept to within two lengths of the lead. Barbaro wasn't even straining; I knew Mr. Silver was history. Then I sensed another horse closing in on us—it turned out to be a colt named Allsmarts, the longest shot in the field at 114–1. I bunched the reins tighter in my hand and made a quick smooching noise, signaling to Barbaro that he could start to run.

The smooch wasn't necessary. Barbaro also sensed the horse approaching and accelerated, as he had in the Laurel Futurity.

Oh. My. God.

As we straightened for home, his ears flattened, he lowered his center even more, and he started reaching so far with his front legs that I felt like I was flying. He quickly left Mr. Silver and Allsmarts behind and moved ahead by three lengths. His ears went up, a sign that he wasn't giving his all, but he had so much momentum that he kept building his lead as we bore down on the finish line. I didn't even bother to look back and see if another horse was gaining on us.

Barbaro was four lengths in front as we hit the finish line. I hadn't whipped him or even showed him my stick.

As we crossed under the wire, I loosened my grip, and Barbaro eased up and slowed down. When he came to a halt, I reached over, patted him on the flank, and spoke encouragingly: "Good boy, way to do your job. You're a hell of a guy."

I could hear the other horses around me blowing like air-conditioning units, worn out from the race. Barbaro was barely breathing hard. He seemed ready for more and disappointed that he had to stop. He glanced back with a quizzical look, as if to say, "That's it? That's all?"

We jogged back around and stopped in front of the grandstand. The Calder fans applauded and shouted Barbaro's name.

Michael and Jose were waiting by the grandstand. Michael had a big smile on his face. We spoke on our way to the winner's circle. I sat on the horse as Jose led him.

"Michael, he sprinted hard for maybe an eighth of a mile at the most," I said. "I didn't get anywhere close to the bottom of him. God, he can run."

I reached down and patted Barbaro's neck. What a first date! I thought to myself that I had probably just ridden the best turf horse of my life. He was just getting started, but what a natural talent. Once he matured, he could probably go anywhere and run on the grass against any horse of any caliber and any age. He could go to the Breeders' Cup, or to historic turf races such as the Prix de l'Arc de Triomphe in France, or England's Epsom Derby. Few American-based horses had ever tried those races, but after what I had just experienced, I thought Barbaro could win them.

"This is an Arc horse," I said to Peter with a smile, "or maybe an English Derby winner."

Peter smiled back. I could tell we thought similarly. I had only been on Barbaro for a couple of minutes, but I started thinking about the history we could make.

Then a few days later Michael called and said he and the Jacksons had made a tough decision. They were taking Barbaro off the turf. From now on, the horse would race on dirt.

To say I was surprised would be an understatement.

CHAPTER 3

From Monterrico to the Top

When I was a boy in Lima, there was no way to imagine the amazing upward arc my life would take. I lived with my parents, seven brothers, and three sisters in a one-room house without electricity. We struggled to put food on the table many nights. What were the chances of a boy from such humble origins becoming a successful jockey in the United States?

My father, Jose, was an obscure racetrack laborer—a foot soldier, not a general. He worked as a groom and assistant trainer at Monterrico, a relatively modern track (opened in 1960) with a compact white-walled grandstand and a sunlit backstretch of concrete and board barns painted red with white trim. My father took care of horses owned by Peru's wealthy sportsmen. He got up at dawn and spent all day sweeping out stalls, filling feed and water buckets, changing bandages, and taking horses to and from the races in the evenings. His wages were small but he loved horses so much he never thought about taking another job. This was what he was meant to do.

While he was at the track, my mother, Zenaida, raised me and my ten brothers and sisters. She was a short woman with a soft voice, a bronze complexion, and dark hair pulled tightly behind her ears. Just seeing her, you wouldn't think she was a tower of strength. But she ruled our family. She was as tough as anyone I've known. She demanded that we live with dignity despite our circumstances. She told us we didn't have to be dirty or act foolishly just because we were poor. We went to school in clothes that were clean and pressed, even if they were hand-me-downs with holes. We worked honest jobs and made do instead of resorting to stealing the many things we didn't have.

Lima—a hectic sprawl of wide streets, big plazas, and old houses with carved balconies, sandwiched between the Pacific Ocean and Andes Mountains—had been the center of South America's Spanish empire centuries earlier, and had a population of four million when I was a boy in the early 1970s. A few people had a lot of money but most were like us, with next to nothing. So many transplants had moved in from the countryside that decent housing, clean water, and electricity were rare.

We lived in the suburban San Luis district. The streets were crowded, but I felt safe. While I went to school, my mother worked a variety of jobs. She washed and ironed other families' clothes, cleaned homes, sold oranges and tomatoes on the street—sometimes all on the same day! The kids helped out when we weren't in school. My older brothers washed cars and swept out houses. I sold tomatoes and Italian ices on the weekends. We took whatever we earned and gave it to my mother, who went to the grocery and came home with dinner. When she didn't have enough money, the grocer advanced her food so we wouldn't go hungry. She always paid him back.

Our house was as simple and flimsy as a child's Lego creation, just one big rectangular room with walls made of concrete blocks and no foundation. There was a kitchen at one end, a den at the other, and everyone slept in the middle on bunk beds. We joked that we slept so closely together that we surely had the same dreams, and that there was so little room that when the sun came in we had to get out.

We ate dinner outside on our version of a porch, a picnic table under a tin roof. When we wanted to watch television after dinner—yes, we had a set—we had to be creative. My father climbed up a light pole outside the house, unscrewed the top of the light fixture, and connected the TV power cord to it. Back inside, we took turns holding the rabbit ears to get better reception. One of us stood by the set holding the rabbit ears in the air as the others shouted, "OK, move to the left! Yes, yes, that's better. No, no, move to the right and hold it higher!" Early the next morning, my father would climb back up the light pole and unscrew the cord before he went to the track.

I had one set of clothes per year—one pair of pants for school, one pair of shoes, a couple of shirts. My mother washed my school clothes every night so it appeared I had more than I did. If I tore up my pants or wore out my shoes,

I either talked a sibling into loaning me a pair or hoped my mother could sew up the damage.

Just about everyone we knew was in the same boat. If I didn't show up for a job sweeping out a house, eight people I knew would volunteer to take my place. You took whatever opportunities came your way, and even if you worked hard, you seldom came home with much money. Sometimes you worked for a sandwich or a drink. Sometimes you didn't get paid at all, just earned a promise of something down the line.

But as hard as those times were, they didn't seem so bad because our family was together, and everyone was trying to do things right. My mother demanded it. She said we weren't going to feel sorry for ourselves. We were going to get up every morning, smile, and keep working to better ourselves.

I was the second youngest of the eleven children, and the youngest of the eight boys. My sister Diana, the oldest of all, and my brothers Juan, Roberto, Anibal, and Jose (children two through five) had it tougher than me. They had to go to school, work, and take care of the younger ones. They lived through the hardest times, when it was just my parents working and we had very little. When an earthquake struck in 1970, my mother shouted to grab the TV—our only possession with any value whatsoever.

We started doing better when the older kids worked. The most dramatic change took place when Anibal became a jockey at Monterrico after he finished high school. All eleven of us grew up going with my father to the track and learning to muck stalls and exercise horses, but only a few eventually worked at the track. Anibal started riding almost out of desperation, to bring in extra money. But he was good at it, and when he started winning, he gave the standard cut to his valet, pocketed just enough for bus fare to and from the track, and handed over the rest to my mother. It made a huge difference. We started eating better and rebuilt our house with better materials and a solid foundation. We fixed up the first floor and added a room for the older boys to sleep in.

In the end, only four of the eleven children wound up in the racing business. Anibal and another brother, Jorge, became jockeys before me. (Jorge was maybe the most talented but he liked to eat too much.) My sister Sara became a groom. Of the others, one drove a taxi, one became a lawyer, one got into the hotel business, one took over a repair shop, one became a carpenter—on and on.

I took to the racing life from the beginning. The horses were so handsome, smart, and fast, and each had its own personality. They awed me. My father loved them so. If anything was wrong with one, he slept in its stall at night to make sure nothing happened. I slept next to him many times. As I got older, I still sold fruit and drummed up whatever jobs I could, but I worked mostly at the track, mucking stalls, walking horses, or cleaning tables in the track kitchen. (I was paid in food there.) My big payoff was the chance to ride. My father put me on a horse when I was six, and I immediately felt at home and looked forward to the days when I could get on one and jog it around the track.

I made good grades as a student at the public San Luis elementary school, excelling in math. I walked a mile and a half to and from the school every day with my sisters Sara and Amalia. I had my dreams. I was going to be a lawyer.

But by the time I was thirteen and enrolled at the crowded, windowless San Luis high school, I had a new dream. I wanted to be a jockey like Anibal and Jorge, who was also riding by then. I yearned for the excitement in their lives.

At first, I kept my dream to myself. Anibal had come home in an ambulance several times, having fallen off a horse and broken various limbs—an arm one time, a leg another. Jorge also came home in an ambulance once. My mother blamed my father, saying, "You took my boys to the track, and look how they came home." It was a sore subject, and I knew she would be upset to hear I wanted to be a jockey, too. She listened to live radio broadcasts of Monterrico racing but had to shut off the sound during the races themselves because she was too worried about what could happen.

But Anibal and Jorge kept riding because it was in their blood—and it was in mine, too. When Anibal heard about my dream, he pulled me aside and said, "OK, but don't do it if you're going to be an idiot and go around smoking and drinking. A lot of jockeys do. They don't last. From where you are now, you can go one of two ways, the right way or the wrong way. If you want to have any kind of a career, you have to go the right way."

I assured him I would. Those other temptations didn't interest me, and I badly wanted to succeed.

Developing my skills to the point that I could ride at Monterrico took years. I had to learn the basics—how to balance myself in the saddle, how to guide the horse, how to use the whip. My father handled most of that. A lifelong horseman, he was wise in all the ways of the track. He taught me to be patient with my horse and pay close attention to it because, he said, every one was different—the best advice I ever got. He set high standards, too. If he didn't like how I galloped a horse, he made me do it again and again until he was satisfied.

Anibal also tutored me. He showed me how to converse with trainers, watch my diet, and work at being fit. He had me walk across the bottom of a swimming pool to strengthen my legs, saying that if I came up for air, he would push me back down. He took me jogging with the other riders. Those lessons really stuck. I'm a fitness fanatic today.

When I was fifteen and a half, I applied to ride. The test consisted of a closed-to-the-public race for young riders seeking their licenses. I won, and the stewards said I could start working. Anibal helped me secure my first mount. I couldn't sleep the night before and arrived at the track hours beforehand, dressed, ready, and beyond excited. I was a jockey!

My horse ran terribly. I finished last. I had never been more disappointed.

It took me a month to win, but I finally did, going wire-to-wire on a colt named Tatin in a six-furlong sprint. The win put me into the apprentice jockey program. I rode with five fewer kilos of weight until I won ten races. Then I gave up a kilo and rode with a four-kilo edge for another ten wins, then three kilos until I won ten more, and so on, until I won fifty races, gave up all edges, and became a full-fledged pro with no advantages.

Most apprentices needed from six months to a year to

compile their fifty wins, but I did it in just three and a half months, a local record. I won two or three races a day and rode in the higher-profile stakes races, usually reserved for veteran riders. Although I went into a slump after I won my fifty races and lost my weight advantage, I soon recovered and started winning again.

My days were jam-packed. I got up early and went to the track with my father to exercise horses in the morning. Then I jogged three miles home, showered, changed into my school clothes, and ran to school to take classes all afternoon. As soon as the bell rang, around 5:30 p.m., I sprinted for the bus that took me to Monterrico, which raced a full card in the evenings. There was no time to spare. If I was riding in the first race, I wore my riding pants under my school pants all afternoon so I didn't have to change. After the races, I went home around ten thirty, needing to eat dinner and do home-work. My mother waited up to feed me soup and fruit. I did my homework and passed out.

My grades suffered because I was so tired and busy. I made it through my sophomore year because my sisters helped me with my homework, and a couple of teachers were racing fans and helped me in exchange for betting tips. But I didn't think I could keep going. I told Anibal I was quitting school to become a full-time rider.

"You are *not* quitting school," Anibal said. "You might get injured and not be able to ride. Then you'll have nothing. Don't be stupid. An education is something you can take through your whole life."

My mother backed him up, and that settled it: I stayed in

school until I graduated. But meanwhile, my riding career took off. I was the second leading rider at Monterrico in my first year as a pro, trailing only Julio Pezua, a twenty-six-year-old veteran who dominated. Then Pezua left to ride in the United States, and I became the top rider. I was winning left and right, in demand, had major stables offering me contracts—all at age seventeen.

Anibal continued to counsel me. He saw my potential and wanted me to fulfill it. He took me aside after races, told me what I had done right and wrong, and encouraged me to have my own style.

From the beginning, I seemed to know which horses needed a tight hold, which needed more freedom—how each ticked. I guess I was meant to be a jockey. Today I can spend five minutes with a horse in a post parade and tell you its strengths, weaknesses, likes, and dislikes, and I was on my way to being able to do that when I was seventeen. I realized that if I saw *after* a race that I should have given a horse more speed early on, it was too late, because the race was over. I needed to know *before* the race. So I studied my horses when I got on them—read them, listened to them. When you take your car to a garage, most mechanics just connect it to a machine that tells them what is wrong. But the best mechanics turn on the car and listen, knowing what different sounds mean. A good jockey has the same skill. He can listen to a horse breathe, feel him as he moves, and know what to do.

I hadn't thought seriously about moving to America and trying to make it. Monterrico was booming, and there was plenty of money to be won. (That would soon cease to be the case.) Few Peruvian jockeys before Pezua had made the jump. But then Juan Manuel Humbert, an owner whom I knew, received videotapes of races at American tracks in California and New York, and he let me sit in his barn and watch them. I spent hours there, studying the higher caliber of American racing and the clever moves of Angel Cordero and Laffit Pincay, Spanish-speaking jockeys who had gone to America when they were young. Humbert said I should go myself if I was so fascinated.

I had mixed emotions. I had met my future wife, Liliana. She was dark-haired, slim, and attractive, and had a smile that lit up a room. We were getting serious. She had come from a better-off family and attended private school, but, like me, she had grown up around racing. Her father was a vet, her godfather a major trainer. We had similar approaches to life and similar personalities, fairly quiet and reserved. But we could talk all day, just the two of us. I hated to leave her.

Humbert gave me another reason to stay when he offered me a $7,000-a-month contract to ride strictly for him—most people in Lima didn't make $7,000 in a year. But I turned him down. I was young and confident and had already conquered Peru as a jockey. I was up for a new challenge. I decided to go.

I left Peru for Miami in 1986, at age eighteen, accompanied by Julio del Castillo, a Peruvian businessman and racing fan who had helped Pezua get established in Miami several years earlier, and connected me with Manny Azparua, a trainer who signed my visa papers and gave me a start. I rode a few horses for Manny at Calder, finishing second the first four times. Finally, I won my first American race on a horse named Single Love on June 1, 1986.

Manny used other riders and encouraged me to ride for other trainers, but I didn't speak English, didn't have an agent, and didn't find much work. One guy said he was willing to become my agent, but he promised to meet me at the track one day and never showed up. I was at the bottom of the jockey ladder.

Mostly, I worked in the mornings as an exercise rider. I was living in Julio del Castillo's apartment in Miami Beach, thirty miles from Calder, and didn't have a driver's license, so I had to get up at 3:00 a.m., catch a bus, change to another bus in North Miami Beach, get off the second bus a mile from Calder, and walk the rest of the way to the track. After my morning work I stayed all day, even if I didn't have mounts in the afternoon. I went jogging, found menial work, watched the races, and then tried to hitch a ride to where I could catch the bus home to Miami Beach.

Money was tight. I had made quite a bit in Peru, but I had given some to my parents and left the rest in the bank as an emergency fund. Now I was barely riding, and nothing was coming in. I did anything at the track for cash—rode horses, washed shovels, raked straw. Grooms paid me, sometimes with money, sometimes with just a sandwich. My checking account mostly went in one direction—down.

By the spring of 1987 I was pretty much broke. I was trying to get my legal papers in order so I could keep working, but I kept hiring lawyers who ripped me off. I called Anibal and asked him to send some of the money I had in the bank in

Peru. Then I called him back and asked for more. When I called a third time, I told him if this money ran out, I was coming home.

I stayed in touch with Liliana and my mother, but I couldn't afford a phone and there were no computers, so we did it all by mail. I wrote my mother long letters, and she wrote even longer ones back, encouraging me to stay positive.

"Keep fighting, son," she wrote me. "You have to believe tomorrow will be better."

Her encouragement helped me keep going. Later I realized she would have loved for me to come home and be closer to her, but she never suggested it. She knew I was chasing a dream and trying to make something of myself. I was broke and alone, but I knew people were rooting for me, and it was exciting to be in America. I was trying hard. And I had a roof over my head.

My fortunes changed when a respected agent named Victor Sanchez took me on in the summer of 1987. Victor had represented several winning riders and said he had been watching me from afar and admired my work ethic. He thought I had promise. He agreed to "take my book"—talk to trainers on my behalf and arrange my mounts. Then he sat me down and told me I had to change how I rode if I was ever going to succeed.

In Peru, I hadn't needed to be aggressive because I was on the best horses. I rode in straight lines, didn't interfere with anyone, and won anyway. Victor told me, "You can't ride like that here. You have to be more aggressive. When someone is coming through on another horse, you have to move over and close the hole so they can't get through. When some-one is coming on your outside, you have to 'carry them out' [veer out and push them wide]. Be tough. That's the only way you're going to win. The other guys are going to do whatever it takes. You have to do the same."

He was right. I was too soft and nice. Sometimes there would be a hole that two of us would be shooting for, and I would pause to think about the other guy, making sure he was OK, and he would beat me to the hole. I wasn't scared, just concerned for my fellow rider. Victor told me I had to stop thinking like that, put myself first, and be the aggressor who got through that hole.

I just had to be tougher, period. Another jockey, Santiago Soto, had teased me since I arrived, saying I couldn't ride and would never make it. He annoyed me, but I took his abuse until one day, after Victor's lecture, I got in his face and challenged him to a fight. Soto backed down and never said another word. Slowly but surely, I was establishing myself.

I started doing better, winning races, getting mounts. My earnings enabled me to move closer to Calder, into an apartment I shared with four guys. I no longer had to take two buses every morning. I was a great roommate, washed windows, cleaned floors, and kept everything neat—I didn't want them to kick me out if I didn't have enough money for the next month's rent.

Victor took me around and introduced me to trainers. Several liked me but said they wouldn't use me unless I spoke English, which was a problem at that point. I had intended to learn English in school back in Lima, but I never did, and now I regretted it. Spanish was being spoken in the racetrack circles I was traveling in, so my English didn't improve.

I got suspended by the stewards a couple of times for taking Victor's lecture about aggressiveness too literally, but I kept at it, and my big break came in early 1988. Victor recommended me to Bob Klesaris, a respected trainer who was sending sixty horses to Suffolk Downs in Boston for the meet there. I had never ridden for him, but he respected Victor's opinion and offered to pay for my travel, buy me winter clothes, help me find an apartment, and put me on all sixty horses.

It was a great offer, but I didn't take it at first. Another major trainer, John Tammaro, was shipping ten horses to Chicago and wanted me to ride them, and I had said I would. Tammaro had previously wanted me to ride many of his horses in Florida (he had 120 in training), but only if I changed agents to one he liked. I couldn't do that to Victor, so I said no, knowing I was passing up a big opportunity. Tammaro respected that and came back to me with the Chicago offer, which I appreciated, but now a better one had come along. When I explained the situation to Tammaro, he said Klesaris's offer was better, and I should take it. So I went to Boston.

Klesaris had a major impact on me. He wanted his jockeys riding one way and one way only—"saving ground," taking the inside route, hugging the rail at all costs. That was the closest way home, he said.

"When you were young and chasing your brothers and sisters around a table, you went faster if you stayed closer to the table, right?" he asked.

That made sense to me.

I went out and saved ground every chance I could. Sometimes I got caught on the outside, but most of the time I hugged the rail and waited for holes to open in the stretch. Some owners and trainers don't like that style because a rider can get pinned inside and have nowhere to go; they scream at their rider, asking why he didn't go outside and find room to run. But I saved ground with confidence because Klesaris wanted it. He didn't care that sometimes I got pinned in and lost on a horse that should have won. He figured that if I hugged the rail all the time, I would win more than I lost.

Horses that don't win anywhere else end up running at Suffolk, so they tended to fade in the stretch. A lot of holes opened on the rail, and I shot through to win again and again. I was also riding more aggressively after Victor's lecture. The other jockeys didn't like it. Some of them had been there for years and resented me coming in and winning day after day. They started calling the stewards on me and filing complaints, and with my limited English, I couldn't explain myself. I got suspended a lot, which was frustrating. I was winning races but would go home and cry. I was young and didn't understand that not everyone wanted me to succeed.

Still, good things happened in the eight months I was in Boston. I hired a new agent, Steve Rushing, because Victor stayed in Florida. Steve and I got off to a hilarious start when he picked me up at the airport in Boston as a favor to Klesaris; neither of us could speak the other's language, so we just stared and smiled. But we eventually formed a partnership that would last a decade and produce thousands of wins. I also met a lot of trainers who later put me on their horses.

Early in 1989 Klesaris said he was sending thirty horses to Maryland and wanted me to ride them all. I asked if he would buy me more clothes and pay my travel expenses again, and he laughed and said all that was on me now. Still, I made plans to go.

Before I started in Maryland, I went to Peru and married Liliana. We had seen each other a few times but had basically become a long-distance couple, and we were tired of living apart. I went back and got started in Maryland, and Liliana and our infant son, Edgar Jr., soon followed. Klesaris found us an apartment, and we were a family in America for the first time.

From the beginning, my luck was good in Maryland. My first mount was a 35–1 shot named Long Allure. I came from behind to win, the horse paid $69, and everyone asked, "Who is this Prado kid?" When I also won on my only other mount of the day, people started talking about me. By the end of my first week, I had five wins, and Steve Rushing was getting lots of phone calls from trainers.

Kent Desormeaux was the dominant jockey in Maryland then, winning a hundred races a year more than any other rider. We battled, and I had more trouble with the stewards, some of which I deserved. One time I got disqualified in a race, and I didn't think I deserved it, so in the next race I carried Kent out—and out and out and out. It was a crazy stunt, and I thought they might take my license away, but they just suspended me. I took Liliana and Edgar to the beach for a much-needed vacation.

When Kent moved to California to ride, I became the king

of Maryland. It wasn't New York, but it was a decent mid-level circuit, and I established myself when top trainers such as Vinnie Blengs and Dale Capuano started putting me on their best horses. Beginning in 1991, I led the state's jockeys in wins for three straight years, and six of the next nine.

I scored my first major victory in October 1991 in the Budweiser International, a turf race at Laurel that attracted horses from around the world. A little French filly named Leariva was entered, but her jockey didn't show up, and I talked the trainer into giving me a shot. I didn't think it would amount to much. Leariva went off at 44–1, and a handful of top jockeys were in the race—Angel Cordero, Laffit Pincay, Jerry Bailey, Chris McCarron. Leariva and I broke from the far outside post, and I rode the rail for as long as I could, but I was pinned in on the far turn and swerved outside. Leariva responded, passed everyone in the stretch, and hit the finish line first.

The win put me on the national map; anyone who hadn't heard of Edgar Prado knew the name now. When Liliana and I moved to a small farm in Howard County, Maryland, in 1993, we named it Leariva Farm. The horse meant that much to us.

Our years at Leariva Farm were marked by momentous events, all positive. Liliana and I became United States citizens in 1993. She gave birth to our daughter Patty in 1993 and our second son, Louis, in 1995. (She also has another daughter, Carolina, from her first marriage.) I had come a long way from the boy who slept in stalls at Monterrico. I was an American, a husband, a father, a property owner. I didn't stop to reflect on my good fortune for long, though—I didn't have time. I was a confirmed workaholic; I loved going to the track to ride in as many races as possible. Steve joked that I never told him no. That work ethic launched my career to a new level in the late 1990s. I continued to ride five days a week in Maryland, but instead of spending days off with my family, I rode at Delaware Park, or in Virginia at Colonial Downs. The pace was exhausting, and I didn't see my family much, but boy, did I pile up the wins. I led the nation with 536 wins in 1997, and again in 1998 with 470 wins.

In 1999 I was on my way to a similar win total when a New York–based trainer, John Kimmel, called and asked me to ride for him at Saratoga that summer. His top jockey was out with an injury. I couldn't say yes fast enough. Saratoga's six-week summertime meet was the major leagues, America's most prestigious meet. The best jockeys competed there.

When Steve Rushing and I arrived, we didn't have a place to stay and didn't even have our names in the condition book, the horsemen's guide that lists the races and all personnel. Other than riding for Kimmel, we were starting from scratch. At first, we just wanted to meet people and start relationships we could turn into business later. But then I won a race, and another, and then shot up the jockey standings. I got close to Jerry Bailey, the leading rider, and wound up second overall, a huge achievement. Established New York jockeys had been coming for years and never finished that high. Here I was from Maryland, doing it the first time.

I had proven myself, and Kimmel asked me to ride for him in the fall meet at Belmont Park in New York. I went there instead of back to Maryland, and finished second in the standings. Then Kimmel asked me to ride at Gulfstream Park in Florida that winter, and we won a lot of races there. In the spring of 2000 I made a big decision. It was time to move permanently to New York—the big stage.

That fall I secured the mount on Lemon Drop Kid, a colt that had won the Belmont the year before and turned into a nice older horse. We won four major races in a row. I was on my way. That fall I won my first riding title at Belmont.

By then I had a new agent booking my mounts. Steve Rushing and his wife were starting a family, and after a decade in Maryland, Steve wanted to stay there. I understood and asked Steve, by now one of my closest friends, to find me a new agent. He put me in touch with Bob Frieze, a well-connected veteran coming off a fifteen-year run as the agent for Jerry Bailey. We met, hit it off, and went to work. Like Steve, Bob soon learned that I seldom said no.

These days I'm in New York most of the year, riding at Aqueduct, Belmont, and Saratoga, with a break for the Gulfstream meet in the winter and also occasional trips to major races elsewhere. It's unusual when a Triple Crown or Breeders' Cup race goes off without me. When I was dominating Maryland in the late 1990s, I lost the mounts on good horses that moved up in class to run in the big leagues; their trainers wanted the best, not some local guy. Now I'm on the other end of those opportunities.

I have won more big races than I can count, including the Belmont Stakes, the Travers Stakes, the Kentucky Oaks, the Haskell Invitational, and many more, along with enough races on a day-to-day basis that in 2004 I became just the nineteenth jockey in history to compile 5,000 wins. I'm lucky. Many people at the racetrack don't enjoy their work; they're in it for the money and can't wait to go home. Not me. Riding is my job, but I enjoy every aspect of it—the competition, the people, the incredible horses. Admittedly, I'm blessed with gifts that have allowed me to succeed, but just as it takes two currents, positive and negative, to light a bulb, it takes two qualities, talent and attitude, to become a successful rider. I have the attitude to support my talent. I go to work with a smile, enjoy my day, and go home with a smile. This is what I was meant to do.

CHAPTER 4

The Saddest Phone Call

Some top jockeys don't want to exercise horses in the mornings because they think they're above it. I love to do it. When I was struggling in my first years in America and morning work was all I had, I lived in fear of trainers and grooms saying, "Sorry, we don't need you today." I heard that often, and the memory of being rejected left a permanent mark. I learned to appreciate every opportunity, big or small. Today, if a trainer asks me to work a horse, instead of telling him when I can make it, I ask, "When do you want me?" I will never forget the sting of being told I wasn't needed.

Several days after I rode Barbaro for the first time in the Tropical Park Derby on New Year's Day 2006, Michael asked if I wanted to exercise the horse one morning at Palm Meadows, a training center in Palm Beach County where many horsemen who come to Florida for the winter stable their horses. I eagerly accepted the offer. I communicate with a horse every time I ride it, and the more I'm on it, the better we understand and trust each other. Barbaro and I were going to be spending a lot of time together, so this extra time would help us get to know each other.

I also was extremely curious to see the horse run on dirt after Michael and the Jacksons had decided to switch him from turf to dirt racing.

When Michael first asked me what I thought about the switch, I admitted I was disappointed. The horse was just so gifted on the turf; he had the potential to rank with the best ever. But I also said I understood. By switching him, Michael and the Jacksons were pointing him at the Kentucky Derby, thinking he might have what it took to win America's biggest race. And maybe he did. If he ran half as well on dirt as he did on turf, he would be in the ball game. Even though the switch posed a significant challenge, with his natural talent, he could still bloom on dirt.

Michael hadn't picked out Barbaro's first dirt race, but he asked if I wanted to work the horse on the dirt on a Monday morning, nine days after the Tropical Park Derby. Peter ordinarily handled Michael's morning riding, so I was excited about the rare opportunity.

But then, a couple of days before the scheduled work, my sister Amalia called from Peru with bad news: my mother's cancer was worsening. She had been at home, but now she was back in the hospital and really struggling. Aside from the cancer, she was also suffering heart failure. I hung up and made plans to go to Peru as soon as possible. It meant I would miss working Barbaro, but suddenly that didn't seem so important.

The phone call from Amalia was not a surprise. My mother had been fighting cancer for several months. I had been trying desperately to arrange a visa for her so she could come to America and receive medical care, but the U.S. embassy in Lima had repeatedly turned us down. She and my father had previously had visas for a decade starting in 1993, and had spent many months with me and my family. They had seen my kids grow up. But when those visas expired, we couldn't get them extended. I didn't know why. My mother wasn't coming to take someone's job. She was just an elderly woman. I had asked many influential people, including the governor of New York, to write to the embassy on my behalf, but nothing had worked.

I flew from Florida to Lima on a Sunday night and spent the next two days with my mother at the hospital before flying back to Florida to ride. She was still sharp mentally, and we talked for hours. She repeated the advice she had given me for years: "Don't worry about me, Edgar. You need to go out and take care of your family, the people who are depending on you just like you depended on your father and me when you were little."

When I got back to Florida on Tuesday, I called Michael to find out about Barbaro's dirt work.

"Edgar, he handled the dirt really well," Michael said. "Peter was extremely happy with how it went."

Michael said Barbaro's first dirt race would be the Holy Bull Stakes in early February at Gulfstream. The horse would work several times before that, and I told Michael I would love to be on him for any or all of the works, but Michael said

Peter would handle the mornings from now on. They didn't want to tinker with success. That was fine, but I told him if he ever changed his mind, I would love to work the horse.

One morning, Bob and I drove up to Palm Meadows to visit Michael and several other trainers. I wasn't getting on any horses; we just wanted to maintain relationships and take a look at some of the horses we were thinking about riding. I saw Barbaro on the dirt for the first time. Peter was riding him. I stood by the rail and watched him gallop by. I could see why Michael and Peter were excited. His running action was higher than it had been on the turf, as it should be; he picked his legs up, was more upright, and as always, moved with purpose. He seemed to be getting the hang of the new surface, and I was delighted to see it.

Just as I was settling back into my Florida routine, my brother Anibal called from Peru. I could hear the sadness in his voice. "Get on a plane now," he said. My mother had been in the hospital since I left a little more than a week earlier, but her doctors were saying her cancer had spread and there was nothing more they could do. She was coming home from the hospital, Anibal said. She wasn't in pain, so, heartbreakingly, she thought she was doing better. But in reality, she didn't have much time left.

I made plans to fly to Peru early the next day. When I opened my mail that evening, I was surprised to receive a letter from the U.S. embassy in Peru, saying her application for a visa extension finally had been approved. Sadly, it probably had come too late for her to travel to the U.S. and receive medical care, but maybe a miracle would happen.

Later that evening, to my great surprise, my mother called as I was packing. I learned later that she came home, put herself in bed, and said, "Bring me the phone." She called everyone—all of my brothers and sisters, uncles and aunts—and had long talks, discussed the future, dispensed advice.

"You're doing well, Edgar. You take care of everyone, starting with your family," she told me.

"Mom, don't worry, I'll see you tomorrow," I said.

When she finished talking, she told Anibal she was tired and wanted to go to sleep.

"Please stay with me tonight, son," she said. "I don't want to be alone."

Anibal, who had assumed such a strong role in the family, pulled up a chair and sat by her side. She said good night, rolled over, went to sleep, and never woke up.

I got the call at home, before I left for the airport. I couldn't bring myself to tell Patty and Louis that their grandmother had died. (Edgar Jr. was at a flight school in Daytona Beach, studying to be a pilot.) I didn't want them at the funeral. I know some people would have handled the moment differently, but for me, it was better that my kids have memories of her when she was alive and well, instead of in a coffin. So I didn't tell them then. They asked where I was going, and I told them I was going to see her. They gave me get-well cards and told me to tell her they were praying for her. Walking out the door was the hardest thing I have ever done.

I got down to Peru as our family gathered for the funeral. I looked around at all my brothers and sisters. What a great family my mother had raised. It was hard not to think about where we had come from, that one-room house with no electricity.

The funeral was at our home in San Luis. Following Peruvian custom, we put up a tent in the front yard and hosted what amounted to a twenty-four-hour service and wake. Between family members, neighbors, and friends, more than 150 people attended. They prayed, cried, ate, laughed, and slept. I was in a daze, struggling to grasp the finality of it. It hit me hard. I had packed my mother's visa extension papers, which came the day before she died. But instead of giving them to her, I put them in the coffin alongside her.

For the first time, I thought maybe I needed to take a major break from riding. I needed to spend more time in Peru with my brothers and sisters. I had enjoyed a lot of success in racing, but what was the point of making a lot of money if you couldn't share it with the people you loved? I almost called Bob and told him to cancel my mounts for several weeks. I was going to bring Liliana and the kids down and take a break.

But I didn't do it. I talked myself out of it. I told myself I was already sad, and if I had too much time to think, I might really get depressed. I also kept hearing the advice my mother had given me: "You have a family of your own that needs you. Take care of them."

My mother raised us to work hard. When I take a break from racing every December, I'm either talking to Bob on the phone, finding out which trainers are calling and offering mounts, or I'm on the computer, checking race results. I even skip meals, like I do when I'm working. It's not much of a vacation, frankly. Liliana tells me, "Next time, leave your phone and computer at home. You need to relax and recharge like everyone else." She might be right, but racing leaves you behind if you aren't careful. If you let up even for a day because you think you're on top, someone digs a ditch below you, and you fall in and can't get out. I have seen it happen to many talented riders. The sport never cuts you slack—and it certainly doesn't wait for you to resolve your personal issues.

The best thing for me to do, I decided, was just go back to work and lose myself in that. I knew I would be sad, but I figured it would help to have something else to think about. I also knew my mother would want me working rather than sitting around missing her. I called Bob and told him I would be back as planned, several days after the funeral, to resume my normal workload at Gulfstream.

When I got back, I broke the news to Patty and Louis. They literally crumbled, just fell to the ground crying. They had been so close to my mother, and like everyone in the family, couldn't imagine life without her.

The next few months were going to be rough.

CHAPTER 5

"I Like Him *That* Much"

At first, I really struggled when I went back to work. I fell apart every time I thought of my mother, and I was reminded of her seemingly everywhere I turned—by seeing her pictures on the wall, by hearing a song she had liked on the radio, by driving past a beach we had gone to with the kids.

When I was at Gulfstream, I made sure I didn't show what I was going through. My mother's death had been reported in the local papers and the *Daily Racing Form*, and unfortunately, some people were liable to see me lose a race and say, "Look, he's not focused. His mind is elsewhere." I worried that if I showed what was inside, some people would use it against me. So I didn't show any emotion until I got home. Then I let everything out behind closed doors, with my family around me. Day after day, I woke up, put on a mask, and went to Gulfstream, came home, fell apart, went to sleep, woke up, put the mask back on, and did it all again.

It helped to receive dozens of condolence letters—from total strangers as well as friends. It was nice to know I had so many people thinking of me. It also helped that the Holy Bull Stakes was coming up in a few days. Although I was getting on and off half a dozen horses a day, I found myself thinking about Barbaro often. With his talent and demeanor, he stood out from the crowd. Anyone who works with horses knows the chance to be around a truly good one is a rare and special privilege. I could hardly wait to spend more time with him.

Of course, he wasn't the only talented three-year-old I was riding that winter. I try to get on as many good ones as possible early in the year, and then Bob and I monitor their development (or lack of it) through the winter and early spring and pick what we think is the best one for me to ride in the Kentucky Derby in May. Some years, our luck runs hot and I have a choice between several promising mounts; other years, we're not as fortunate and I get stuck on a Derby long shot. At this early point, the beginning of February, 2006, was shaping up as a good year. I had the mount on several three-year-olds that handicappers and experts considered legitimate Derby contenders.

The one with the best résumé was First Samurai, a colt that had been among the best two-year-olds of 2005, winning four straight races, including the Champagne Stakes, a prestigious race at Belmont. Jerry Bailey had been his jockey, but he had retired, and the horse's trainer, Frankie Brothers, had selected me as a replacement. I also had the first call on Strong Contender and Bernardini, a pair of talented, injury-prone colts that we thought could develop into Derby horses if they stayed healthy. I might pick up other mounts as the season progressed and hopefully would have options if Barbaro didn't pan out.

The Holy Bull Stakes was held on February 4 as part of a big card at Gulfstream that included the Donn Handicap, a major race for older horses, and the Hutcheson Stakes, another Derby prep race. The Holy Bull actually was the lesser of the day's Derby preps, ranked as a Grade III event while the Hutcheson was a Grade II. (The most prestigious American races are "graded" stakes, and the lower the grade, the bigger the race. Triple Crown and Breeders' Cup races are Grade I events, as are the biggest Derby preps.) The slate of races should have attracted one of the biggest crowds of the Gulfstream meet, but a hard rain started falling the day before and never stopped. The track turned brutally sloppy, and fewer than eight thousand fans came out.

Long ago I got used to riding in rainy weather, although I certainly don't prefer it. There's mud flying everywhere, and you're soaked and filthy by the end of every race. Your valet really earns his pay, washing a couple sets of clothes as the day goes on so you always have clean ones to change into for the next race.

Then there is the goggle issue. I start every race with a pair of plastic goggles covering my eyes and three or four other pairs positioned on my face, above my eyes. I need goggles to protect my eyes from the dirt that the other horses throw up in the air as they run, but the first pair is usually caked with dirt in fifteen or twenty seconds, so I slide them down around my neck, then raise my hand and pull down a replacement pair. I do it so quickly that most fans never see the switch, but in fact, I use three or four pairs during a normal race on a dry track. On a sloppy track I need more, and on the day of the Holy Bull Stakes I shuffled through goggles as rapidly as an expert poker player shuffled through cards, using five or six pairs per race.

The track itself was fairly firm despite the water pooling on the surface. Gulfstream's owners had recently poured millions of dollars into a renovation of the entire facility, including the racing surfaces, and in truth, the dirt track wasn't that slippery. A track record would fall in the Donn Handicap later in the day.

Still, Michael didn't really want Barbaro's dirt debut to come on such an "off" track, and he considered scratching the horse as rain fell all day. But after discussing that option with Peter, who said Barbaro would be fine, he finally decided to run him. I wasn't concerned, either. In my experience, horses that run well on the turf also tend to do well in the slop because their feet go through the dirt and hit the "bottom" of the track, the cushion underneath the surface, which is soft, like grass.

Before I got on Barbaro, though, I rode First Samurai in the Hutcheson Stakes. This was his 2006 debut, and racing fans were excited to see him. He had the lowest odds (7–1) of any individual horse in the Kentucky Derby Future Book, an advance betting pool run by Churchill Downs, and he went to the starting gate in the Hutcheson as a big favorite at 3–5. He had won the Champagne Stakes on a sloppy track the previous fall.

I was on him for the first time, and my first impression was positive: physically, he was solid and muscular, and he acted like a pro in the post parade. He loaded into the starting gate without incident and broke well.

The race was short, just 7 1/2 furlongs, around one turn. Another horse beat us to the early lead—a colt named Keyed Entry, the second betting choice at 3–1, trained by Todd Pletcher and ridden by Johnny Velazquez. Pletcher had Gulfstream's biggest and best stable, and Velazquez, a native of Puerto Rico who had won more big races than any jockey in the country in 2004 and 2005, was Pletcher's number-one rider.

Johnny positioned Keyed Entry wide of the rail as he came up the backstretch because the track was especially sloppy inside. I was right on his heels, one length back. With the race being so short, I moved for the lead on the turn, but when I tried to swing First Samurai around Keyed Entry, the other horse was up to the challenge. Johnny asked him to respond, and he refused to let First Samurai pass. We swung into the home straightaway and dueled down the stretch, leaving the other five horses in the field far behind. The pace was so hot that the track record for 7 1/2 furlongs fell, and the third-place finisher was sixteen lengths back. I put the whip to First Samurai and thought we would pass Keyed Entry, but our competitor showed a lot of heart and fought us off. First Samurai couldn't gain ground. Keyed Entry was one and a quarter lengths ahead at the finish.

Frankie Brothers wasn't disappointed. He had wanted to win, but considering that First Samurai hadn't raced since November, it wasn't a bad performance.

"I thought he ran well for his first start off the bench in three months," Frankie told the press.

That was the eighth race of the day, and the Holy Bull Stakes immediately followed. Its field didn't have horses like First Samurai that had accomplished so much as two-year-olds; of the twelve entries, Barbaro, with his three turf wins, had done the most. He was the 3–2 favorite.

A driving rain fell as I showered, quickly changed into the Jacksons' silks, and went to the paddock. Just like before the Tropical Park Derby, Barbaro was antsy and snappy until Michael saddled him, and then he calmed down. He always seemed to understand that it was time to buckle down when Michael tightened the girth underneath him.

Michael helped me up and onto the horse. I spoke gently to him and patted his long, muscular neck, letting him know we were in this together. Barbaro knew I liked him. Horses can sense emotions like that. It's a silent communication—how you look at him, how you hold the reins, how you pat him.

When I get on horses that don't like me, I don't fight them. If you're wrestling with one another, you're not going to win. If a horse wants to buck a little, I let it buck. If it wants to kick a little, I let it kick. I let it know I'm there, and it respects that, but I don't have to be in control. I don't think you can be in control of a horse. It is bigger and stronger, and if it wants to do something, it does. You have to respect that.

Every horse has a key that makes it happy, makes it run faster. You have to find that key. Does it want to race in front, in the middle of the pack, or in back? Does it like to be hit right-handed, left-handed, or not at all? Some horses are easy to figure out, and some are complicated. They aren't cars; they have minds of their own. It's like with kids, how some like music, some like baseball, and some like soccer. With horses, some want to run only on grass or on dirt, or in certain weather, or with certain shoes.

Horses like Barbaro make my job easy. He didn't have keys. He was unlocked! I spoke to him, said, "Take me to the magic throne, big guy," and he relaxed and came to me. I sang to him, whatever came to mind. All animals respond to voices emotionally, and Barbaro really did. He knew I was happy on him and confident in him. I played with his ears, patted him, and he looked around like an athlete that knew he was going to win.

Before we left the paddock for the Holy Bull Stakes, Michael didn't give me instructions. Like all the best trainers, he never gave instructions, just wished me luck. What was the point of giving instructions? A good jockey doesn't need them, and a bad jockey can't follow them. You can tell a rider to lie here and follow another horse there, but when the starting gate opens, the race almost never unfolds as planned. A jockey just has to react to what develops. The good ones react well.

Rain fell so hard during the post parade that I heard drops hitting puddles with a *pop-pop-pop* sound. It was strangely quiet otherwise, with many of the fans having found shelter somewhere on the grounds, away from trackside. Most horses don't mind running in the rain, but a few hate getting wet, and you can easily spot them during the post parade—they get bug-eyed and agitated.

Barbaro wasn't the least bit upset. He went into the starting gate without a hitch and came out running hard as soon as the gates sprang open. I settled him just behind the early leader, a colt named Doctor Decherd that had won a stakes race a month earlier. I was curious to see how Barbaro's running action changed on the new surface. As I expected, it was quite different—he was "climbing" with his front legs, bringing them up and down rather than throwing them out like a broad jumper at a track meet. He wasn't covering quite as much ground with every step, but considering the slop and the new surface, he was moving along at a nice clip.

The distance of the race was $1\frac{1}{8}$ miles, covering two turns. We were a couple of lengths back as we went around the first turn, but I slowly crept up on Doctor Decherd all the way up the backstretch. Another colt named Flashy Bull was pressuring me from the outside, but Barbaro was focused solely on the leader. I chirped at him, telling him to move, and he pulled even with Doctor Decherd as we headed into the second turn. By the middle of the turn, he had poked his head in front for the lead.

This was the place where he had moved in his other races, but he didn't have the same burst of acceleration this time. He even eased up for a moment when he took the lead, allowing Doctor Decherd to come back and recapture the lead inside of us. Barbaro responded, picked up his pace, and poked his head back in front as we straightened into the home stretch.

With Flashy Bull still just behind us and Doctor Decherd hanging on, we had a fight on our hands. There would be no runaway sprint this time. Barbaro had to dig in and grind out a lead coming down the stretch. To make sure he was focused, I pulled out my whip and gave him a pair of jolts, one on his left flank and one on his right. He got the message, crept away from Doctor Decherd, and pulled ahead by a length.

With an eighth of a mile to go, he had a clear lead of two lengths. Doctor Decherd and Flashy Bull hung around, though, staying close enough to rally if Barbaro faltered. And then, out of nowhere, another horse came flying at us, making a late run. I didn't know who until I got back to the jockeys' room and watched the replay—it was Great Point, a 25–1 shot. He'd got caught in traffic early and was running last for the first half mile, but after he veered outside and found running room, he started passing horses like crazy.

As Great Point rallied out in the middle of the track, Barbaro rolled along, distracted by a string of TV lights hung from the finish line. He was racing at slightly less than top gear, and Great Point bore down on us from five lengths back, then four, then three. He passed Doctor Decherd and Flashy Bull, and took aim at us. I pulled the whip back out and hit Barbaro again, once on the left side and once on the right.

Barbaro didn't know the other horse was there until Great Point veered inside and closed to within a length of us as we neared the wire. Sensing the challenge and feeling the sting of my whip, Barbaro snapped out of his daydream, forgot about the TV lights, and started to run. We hit the finish line three-quarters of a length in front of Great Point. Barbaro had won his fourth straight race without a defeat, and his first on dirt.

No doubt, this had been tougher than the Tropical Park Derby, but once again, Barbaro was barely breathing hard as I slowed him down and brought him to a halt. He could have gone on. In fact, he ran harder after he crossed the finish than just before. It was like finding out that your car had an extra gear.

Michael was waiting with a smile when I got back to the grandstand. He was happy, but he immediately asked, "Would that other horse have passed you if the race had been longer?" Some fans and handicappers would later suggest Great Point, indeed, would have passed us in a longer race. But they obviously didn't keep watching after the finish. Barbaro pulled back away. He had more than enough left in the tank and wasn't about to let another horse get in front of him. He was too competitive for that.

"No way, Michael," I said. "We could have gone all the way around the track again and we would have stayed in front."

He nodded and asked another question: "What do you think overall? How did he do?"

I thought about what had just happened. Barbaro had showed plenty of speed, showed he could run in the slop, and responded to pressure for the first time; he had looked at those other horses and fought hard to win. He hadn't accelerated as amazingly as he did on the turf, but that was the only negative.

Maybe this wasn't as impressive as his turf wins, but the new surface was a big change, and overall, he had done very well.

"He's getting there, Michael. He's learning," I said.

"Do you think he's better on dirt or turf?" Michael asked.

"I do think he's better on the turf," I said. "But he has passed a big test, so we should move on. We can't turn around and go back now that he has proved he can run on the dirt. He's still learning. I think he will continue to learn and improve."

Michael nodded. He and the Jacksons had already made up their minds to go for the Kentucky Derby. Michael didn't say that then, but he knew what kind of horse Barbaro was. He knew he had a Derby horse if Barbaro performed to his ability.

Later, I spoke to Bob Frieze about the day and some upcoming races. We discussed the Holy Bull Stakes.

"That other horse was really flying at the end. Should we try to get on him?" Bob asked.

"He's no Barbaro," I said. "Barbaro ran great, Bob. He was going to be a turf superstar, and he has started over on the dirt, but he's getting there. He has the potential to be a dirt superstar, too."

"You like him that much?" Bob asked.

"Yes, absolutely," I said. "I like him that much."

CHAPTER 6

The Chosen One

A jockey makes many decisions every day: where to ride, when to ride, who to ride, how to ride. When I look back at my year with Barbaro, I see a couple of decisions that were key forks in the road—decisions that could have kept everything from happening had I gone the other way.

There was, for instance, my decision to keep riding after my mother's death. If I had told Bob I was taking off in late January, I'm sure Michael would have given the mount to someone else, starting with the Holy Bull Stakes. He would have understood my reasoning and surely given me a pass for breaking my promise always to be there to ride the horse, but he would have moved on, and I would have ended up watching Barbaro.

Then there was my decision to make Barbaro my Kentucky Derby mount. He made that call easy by continually winning his races, but I was on enough other talented horses that spring that the logic of going with him wasn't always quite as clear as it seemed in hindsight. I like to think fate intervened.

After the Holy Bull Stakes, Michael charted a relaxed schedule for him in the months leading up to the Derby. Barbaro would take the next eight weeks off—all of February and March, basically—and then, in early April, race in the Florida Derby, the biggest of Gulfstream's Derby preps. If all went well there, the horse would then lay off five more weeks until the Kentucky Derby.

It was an unusual plan. Most trainers pushed their Derby-caliber horses a lot harder. The Derby has twenty horses in the field, as opposed to the seven to twelve that compete in most other races. Given the larger field, it can be a brutal race, with much bumping and jostling, especially in the early going. Most trainers feel a horse needs to be battle-tested to survive, much less win, so they run their Derby candidates in at least three or four preps. But Michael decided Barbaro would race just once in the three months before the Derby. That wasn't much action, especially for a horse still adjusting to a new surface. And it had been fifty years since a horse won the Derby coming off a five-week layoff.

The media had a field day, with some writers questioning whether Michael knew what he was doing. I'm sure some fans had the same doubts. Michael had never trained a Derby horse, had been a Thoroughbred trainer for less than a decade, and hadn't even won a Grade I race until 2003, when Kicken Kris won the Secretariat Stakes, so he was easily second-guessed. But the doubts were misplaced. Having ridden Kicken Kris and several of his other good runners, I knew Michael was a shrewd horseman. Yes, he had his own way of doing things, but who didn't? And I thought his way was smart. He didn't wear his horses out in the mornings; he pushed them just occasionally, saving their best effort for the afternoons. He built up their lungs and rear ends, probably as a holdover from his show jumping days, when he rode horses that had to be strong enough to clear jumps. Horses are like those old Volkswagen cars with the engines in the back—their power comes from the rear. A trainer had to treat that rear like gold, and Michael did.

Michael looked younger than his fifty-five years and had enjoyed much success as a jumper before becoming a trainer, earning a place on three U.S. Olympic teams to go with his half dozen national titles. After winning a team silver medal in show jumping at the 1996 Summer Games in Atlanta, he was selected by the U.S. Olympic Committee to carry the flag at the closing ceremonies. One of the reasons he was chosen was an act of heroism he had performed in 1989, when a United Airlines plane he was on crashed in an Iowa field and burst into flames, killing more than a hundred people. Michael had survived the crash, led three young siblings traveling alone out of the wreckage, and gone back into the flames to save an infant. He was named "Person of the Week" by ABC News.

With his history of rising to occasions, Michael was not to be underestimated. His schedule for Barbaro didn't concern me. He knew he was dealing with a hugely talented horse, and he wanted the horse fresh on the first Saturday in May, not before. Show jumpers can take six months off from competition and come back primed to perform at their best. I had faith that Michael, coming from that background, would have Barbaro perfectly ready.

And of course, I had faith in Barbaro, too. His performance in his first race on dirt had convinced me he could make the transition. It would be a gradual process, but with the Derby still three months away, he had time to adjust. And while he wouldn't be competing much, he would be in good hands, working under Michael and Peter. He would take long gallops on most mornings and work a harder half mile or six furlongs once a week.

While he trained at Palm Meadows during those late winter and early spring months, I rode every day at Gulfstream. I got on the other horses I was considering for the Derby, starting with a colt named Strong Contender trained by John Ward, trainer of the 2001 Kentucky Derby winner, Monarchos. On February 22 I rode Strong Contender in an allowance race (for less accomplished horses). It was just his second start, and despite coming back from a fractured shin, he dominated, winning by four and a half lengths. Ward wasn't sure the colt would have enough experience to run in the Derby, but still hoped to get him there.

On March 4 I rode First Samurai again, this time in the Fountain of Youth Stakes at Gulfstream. It was First Samurai's first start since the Hutcheson Stakes. I thought he would improve, and a lot of other people did, too: he was the 7–10 favorite. I kept him on the rail and in front around the first turn, up the backstretch, and around the second turn. As we turned for home, a colt named Corinthian passed us, and I had to veer outside to make a run. As I began to gain ground,

Corinthian veered out and knocked me into another horse. Corinthian won, but I lodged a protest, and the stewards upheld it, saying Corinthian had interfered. First Samurai was declared the winner.

Win or lose, First Samurai had performed reasonably well in his first longer race around two turns. But was he dominating? No. I took that into account when First Samurai's trainer, Frankie Brothers, and his owner, Bruce Lunsford, asked me after the race to commit to riding the horse in his next two races, tentatively the Blue Grass Stakes, a major Derby prep in Kentucky, and then, hopefully, the Kentucky Derby. I turned them down. Barbaro had more potential, and I wanted to give him time to develop into the racehorse I knew he could be.

Everywhere I turned that spring, I rode Derby-caliber horses. On March 4 I rode Bernardini in a maiden race. Of all the other horses I rode that spring, he impressed me the most. Injuries and illness had kept him from racing much, but he was ready now—really ready—and put on a show, winning by almost eight lengths. Two weeks later I rode Keyed Entry, the colt that had upset First Samurai in the Hutcheson. John Velazquez had given him up to stay on another of Todd Pletcher's Derby contenders, and I stepped in for the Gotham Stakes, a Derby prep at Aqueduct in New York on March 18. We finished second by a neck.

Finally, as March turned to April, it was time to get back on the one horse that had captivated me. I spoke to Michael several times during Barbaro's layoff, asking how he was doing (the answer was always positive) and also if I could work him one morning (the answer was always negative). Now it was time to get on him for the first time in eight weeks, in the Florida Derby on April 1.

The race-day weather was sunny and warm, and a big crowd jammed Gulfstream. With its $1 million purse and history of producing big-name winners, the Florida Derby was an important Kentucky Derby prep race. Barbaro was the 3–2 favorite. The other horses drawing interest included a 6–1 shot named Sharp Humor that had won the Grade II Swale Stakes in his last start.

The undercard was packed with stakes events leading up to the Florida Derby, which was run near the end of the day, at around six. I could hardly wait to get to the main event. Barbaro and I had competed just twice together so far, but I felt we were forming a meaningful bond. I had such confidence in him, and conveyed that to him by being relaxed on his back and letting him race at his own pace and with his own style. An intelligent horse reacts to the people around him, reads their moods, and understands what they represent. He knew that my presence, combined with the noise of a racetrack crowd and his being in a paddock, meant he was getting ready to run—and run hard, unlike at Palm Meadows. He trusted me to guide him with respect, and to really let him let loose when the time was right.

A jockey doesn't spend as much time with a horse as its trainer or exercise rider, but the experience of racing together in front of thousands of screaming fans can't be duplicated in training. It brings you together. You give them a pat, speak to them, and they know who you are and wait for you to tell them what to do. Barbaro was a dream to ride. He knew his business. And he was fast.

A half hour before the Florida Derby, Barbaro was being wetted down in an outdoor holding paddock. Michael was running a sponge over his back when a drop of water landed on Barbaro's foot. The sensation spooked him, and he lashed out with his right rear leg—a cow kick, it's called—and caught Michael in the upper right arm. The blow was delivered with such force that Michael was knocked back ten feet. His head smacked into the back wall of the paddock. Michael was still shaken when we met in the main paddock a few minutes later. Getting kicked is part of the job when you work with horses, but a long, dark bruise had already come up, and Michael wondered if he had suffered a broken arm. (He would go to the hospital for X-rays the next day, but they were negative.) He was thankful the incident hadn't happened in the main paddock, where TV cameras would have caught it.

As frightening as it was, the kick was an excellent example of Barbaro's raw athleticism. He lashed out with a cat's quickness, yet also with a tank's steamrolling power. There was nothing slow and dull about him. He was a running machine unmatched in strength and reflex.

Before I got on Barbaro, I discussed tactics with Michael and Peter. Michael was worried about the extreme outside post he had drawn—No. 10 in an eleven-horse field. The distance from the starting gate to the first turn was just a sixteenth of a mile in a 1⅛-mile race at Gulfstream, and few horses won from the outside posts because they got stuck outside and had to run the whole race wide of the rail, or got caught in early traffic and pushed to the back of the pack. Either scenario could cost us the race.

I would have been more concerned if I had been on another horse coming out of the No. 10 hole, but Barbaro was very nimble for being so big. He always came out of the gate quickly, running hard. Many horses his size acted like they were standing in molasses before they got going.

"He will take us where we need to go," I told Michael. "We'll be fine."

Peter wasn't concerned about the post, either, but he was worried about Sharp Humor, a colt I had ridden three times (winning twice) as a two-year-old in New York. Sharp Humor had plenty of speed and looked to be improving. Peter feared him starting fast and getting so far ahead that we couldn't catch him.

Peter helped me up and onto Barbaro. I was determined to do well. Johnny Velazquez was having a big day in front of the big crowd, having already ridden several winners. Michael looked at me and said, "Let's put an end to that and win the Derby."

"Sounds good to me," I said as I rode off.

After an uneventful post parade, Barbaro was one of the last horses loaded into the starting gate. When the gate opened and the horses burst out, he bobbled on his front ankles and bumped into the horse inside of us as he tried to get going. In the stands, Michael's heart probably jumped into his throat. But the bump didn't faze Barbaro. Sharp Humor jumped into the lead, but Barbaro found his stride and shot past most of the rest of the field before the first turn. I marveled again at his blend of size and quickness. We were second, close to the rail, as we went around the first turn, and Michael said later that the first sixteenth of a mile probably was the key to the race.

Barbaro was still climbing more than gliding, but this was his first race on a fast dirt track, so he was still feeling his way. And don't get me wrong, other horses would be lucky to move so well at any point in their dirt careers. As we turned up the backstretch, he was galloping easily and I had a relaxed hold on the reins. I briefly bunched them and tugged, just to see what I had, and Barbaro immediately responded, so I loosened him up again. I knew he would be there when I called on him.

Even without my asking him to go, he crept closer and closer to Sharp Humor all the way up the backstretch. We were no more than a neck behind as we curved into the second turn. So much for any concerns about Sharp Humor running away.

Another horse was pressing us from the outside—a 35–1 shot named Sam's Ace, I learned later. I thought it was time for Barbaro to go, so I chirped at him. He pulled even with Sharp Humor on the turn, but he didn't surge into the lead, as he had always done before. Sharp Humor hung right with him along the rail. His jockey, Mark Guidry, was really whipping him.

We were neck-and-neck coming out of the turn, looking at the quarter-mile run to the finish. Barbaro's attention went in and out. He took the lead with a couple of strong strides, but then, just like in the stretch of his prior race, he seemed to get distracted by the TV lights hanging from the finish line in the distance, and Sharp Humor came back at him. That surprised him, for sure—no horse had ever come back on him after being passed—and I took out the whip and gave him a sharp rap. He snapped out of his daydream, took several long strides, and regained the lead. But then he eased up again, probably because of the lights, and Sharp Humor caught us, nudged past us, and regained the lead at the eighth pole.

I whipped Barbaro a second time, and he responded, quickly pulling even. Later, people asked if I was concerned he might lose. I wasn't. Whenever I whipped him, he snapped to attention and went right by Sharp Humor. He was playing around, being a kid, and seemingly could accelerate almost instantly. I wasn't being too hard on him. Actually, I was pleased to see his competitive spirit: it quite obviously bothered him to have another horse pass him. He dug in and ran harder every time.

At the eighth pole, I whipped him again and he sped up enough to get back in front by a neck. As we headed for the wire, Sharp Humor didn't have enough left to come back a third time, and Barbaro kept pushing. We hit the finish line in front by the length of Barbaro's head. Sharp Humor had pushed us all the way to the wire. But we were the winners. And no one else was close.

Barbaro was again barely blowing as he eased up, though this had easily been his hardest race. He wanted to keep going. I couldn't believe it. What would it take to tire him?

Later, some fans and reporters would cast a negative light on his performance, saying he had to go all out to beat a lesser horse. When I was asked about it, I explained that he had been distracted by the TV lights and, despite the close call, actually had plenty of gas left in the tank. I thought it was a terrific performance, just his second race on dirt. He had looked Sharp Humor straight in the eye, battled for a quarter mile, and showed he wanted to win. I thought the race would sharpen his mind for racing and make him even better.

When I brought the horse back around to the foot of the grandstand, the fans cheered, and everyone on Barbaro's human "team" was waiting with big smiles. Jose took him from me, clipped on the lead shank, and held him. Roy Jackson reached up, shook my hand, patted the horse on the right side of his neck, and said, "Good boy, way to run." His pride was obvious. Gretchen Jackson also came over, congratulated me, and petted Barbaro.

Roy took the shank and walked the horse to the winner's circle. When a track official tried to drape a blanket of pink and white orchids across Barbaro's neck, the horse ducked his head and shrugged it off. He didn't want any part of the flowers. After the win picture was taken, I got off and the press descended on us. Barbaro was obviously headed for the Kentucky Derby now, and Michael fielded a lot of questions about giving him such a long layoff before the big race. Michael pointed out that Barbaro hadn't raced in eight weeks before this race today.

"And he was ready to run today," Michael said. "I'm no more concerned [going to the Derby] than I was about the eight-week layoff. I just think he's a good horse."

As the reporters milled around, I stood by Peter, who commented that this race should make a man out of Barbaro. The horse had come in a boy, he said, and was a man now after being challenged and whipped and learning that sometimes he had to fight to win. I agreed.

Gretchen Jackson came over and quietly asked me the big question: Did I want to ride the horse in the Kentucky Derby? I knew that was coming and was sure I did, but I hemmed and hawed, as any veteran jockey would. The Derby prep season wasn't over. I was still booked to ride Keyed Entry in the Wood Memorial a week later, and Strong Contender in the Blue Grass Stakes in mid-April. If I committed to Barbaro now, I might lose those mounts, because the trainers might prefer to go with a jockey who could also commit to riding their horses in the Kentucky Derby.

I smiled and said to Gretchen, "I love your horse, but I'm still thinking about it. I still have a couple of other horses to ride in other races. I need to check out all of my options."

My "indecision" was based largely on economics. The Blue Grass and Wood Memorial each had a $750,000 purse, of which 60 percent, or $450,000, would go to the winner. (That percentage holds for most races in the United States.) A jockey makes 10 percent of what the horse earns, so I would make $45,000 if I won one of the races. After giving the industry-standard 25 percent to my agent and another 5 percent to the valet, I could pocket more than $30,000. That was worth shooting for, even on a horse that wasn't my Derby mount.

Many jockeys who are fortunate enough to have options around Kentucky Derby time hold off on committing for as long as they can—it's just business, nothing personal, and Gretchen knew that. She was wonderfully understanding. She didn't demand that I immediately make a decision about Barbaro, but rather just repeated that they would love to have me ride him.

As we were leaving the winner's circle, a reporter approached and asked if Barbaro was my Kentucky Derby horse. I said I really liked him, but still hadn't made up my mind. Peter looked at me with a smile. "You've got to be crazy if you don't ride this horse in the Derby," he said. Barbaro was a top Derby contender. My other mounts weren't in his class.

When I spoke to Michael, I said I wanted to ride in the other races before I committed to Barbaro for the Derby. He said he would give me one week to make a decision, and then, if necessary, start looking for another jockey. I knew we wouldn't get that far.

The Wood Memorial was run in New York a week later. Keyed Entry was the favorite, and I put him in front around the first turn and up the backstretch, but he lacked a finishing kick and ended up third. I felt he belonged in shorter races and knew he wasn't my Derby mount. (He ran in the Kentucky Derby, but finished last.)

Michael made calls to several other jockeys' agents shortly before the Wood, asking if their riders would be available to get on Barbaro in the Kentucky Derby. Agents talk to each other constantly, and Michael knew word would get back to Bob that he was starting to look around. Just like I was playing my game, he was playing his. Fair enough, business as usual in the racing world.

As I left the track after the Wood and headed for the jockeys' room, a reporter approached and asked if I had picked my Derby mount. I nodded and said, "Yes, I'm going to ride Barbaro."

And, I thought to myself, we're going to win.

CHAPTER 7

"This Is the Derby Winner"

Shortly after the Florida Derby, Barbaro was shipped to Kentucky. With Michael and Peter monitoring his every step, he resumed training at Keeneland Race Course, the historic track in Lexington where coats and ties are still a clubhouse requirement and until relatively recently there was no track announcer, so all you heard during a race was the pounding of hooves, like in the old days. The track's spring meet was in full bloom, so it was crowded with horses and people. Barbaro floated under the radar. He galloped every morning and worked just once, covering five furlongs in a minute and 1 2/5 seconds—not exceptionally fast. Michael wasn't about to burn him out.

People in Kentucky had succumbed to Derby fever, as they do every spring. The big race was in three weeks, then two weeks, then just a matter of days. Talk of Derby horses and Derby strategy was heard in the barns and grandstands. Derby articles dominated the local papers and the horse racing press.

Barbaro was just one of the many quality horses with legitimate credentials being primed for the big race. The other top contenders included Brother Derek, a front-running colt that had won three Derby prep races in California; Lawyer Ron, winner of six races in a row, including three Derby preps at Oaklawn Park in Hot Springs, Arkansas; Sweetnorthernsaint, a naturally fast colt coming off a nine-and-a-quarter-length win in the Illinois Derby; Sinister Minister, a blazing-fast runner that had won the Blue Grass Stakes by an astounding twelve and three-quarters lengths; and Bob and John, come-from-behind winner of the Wood Memorial.

Barbaro had never raced against any of them, but I thought he had more going for him. He was undefeated in five starts at four tracks (Delaware Park, Laurel, Calder, and Gulfstream) on three surfaces (grass, dirt, and slop). That meant he hadn't just dominated one set of horses at one track, as some of the others had during the prep season. He certainly had the pedigree to handle the Derby's 1¼-mile distance, unlike some of the others. And he had that awesome finishing kick.

I read several writers' analyses of how the race likely would be run. There was little doubt Sinister Minister and Keyed Entry would share the early lead and set a hot pace. The faster they went, the better the race shaped up for "closers" coming from behind in the stretch. Barbaro was one of those. My goal was to keep him behind the early leaders, but not too far behind, and then let him loose turning for home. That was how he had won his prior races, and even though the twenty-horse field raised the possibility of traffic trouble, I saw no reason to change tactics now.

When each contender's pros and cons were listed in the articles, Barbaro's biggest drawback was the five-week pre-Derby layoff. Some writers (and some horsemen) thought Michael was blowing it by not having Barbaro sufficiently battle-tested. Michael was not happy about the second-guessing. He kept his temper in check publicly, but a horseman hates nothing more than to have other people think they know what is best for his horse. He knew Barbaro best, and knew what the horse needed to be ready.

I was riding in New York for most of the month, but I also had mounts at Keeneland, so I spent several days there, saw Barbaro, and spoke to Michael and Peter. They told me he was training perfectly. The last thing I wanted was to tell Michael how to do his job, but I did have one concern. As part of a twenty-horse field, Barbaro surely would have dirt kicked in his face by horses running in front of him. Some horses hate that, balk, and refuse to run hard. I didn't know how Barbaro would respond because he had raced only twice on dirt and behind just one or two horses, so he hadn't taken much dirt to the face.

"Whatever you do, Michael, please make sure he is used to taking the dirt," I said.

I didn't want any surprises. If Barbaro stumbled out of the gate and wound up farther back than I wanted in the early going, he would take a lot of dirt, and if he didn't like it, he might fight me and struggle to gain ground. That meant he would expend more energy early, leaving him with less for the stretch.

Michael assured me the issue was covered. "Don't worry,

Edgar," he said. "We've taught him all about the dirt. He handles it great. It doesn't bother him at all."

One afternoon I saw Peter in the paddock at Keeneland before a race and, before I got on my horse, went over to speak to him specifically about the dirt. Peter said he had spent a lot of time exercising Barbaro "in company," with another horse throwing dirt back. He confirmed there was no reason to worry.

"He's just so darn big and strong," Peter said with a smile. "He's looking down at the horses in front of him, and when dirt gets thrown back at him, he barely pays attention."

As the Derby neared, I became more and more excited about Barbaro's chances. I had ridden in the Derby every year since 2000, but had never won. My best finishes had been a third and a fourth. As much as I had accomplished overall in racing, I hadn't left much of a mark on the Derby. But Barbaro, I believed, was my best chance ever.

My previous best chance had come in 2002 on a colt named Harlan's Holiday that won the Florida Derby and Blue Grass Stakes and went off as the Derby favorite. He was a big, strong colt that could run on the lead or come from behind, and accelerated almost as sharply as Barbaro. My mother, Liliana, and Patty came to Louisville because I wanted my family there when I won the Derby, and Harlan's Holiday seemed to have a great shot. If the Derby had been run in March, he would have won. But he had peaked too soon. He ran seventh in the Derby.

The next year, I was on a quality colt named Peace Rules that had the lead turning for home. But he had used up too much of his energy chasing a frontrunner early in the race; he liked being on the lead himself, was annoyed to see another horse ahead of him, and fought me the whole way, wanting to go faster. Two horses passed us in the stretch, and we finished third.

Otherwise, I hadn't done anything in the Derby, finishing seventeenth on Commendable in 2000, fourth on Thunder Blitz in 2001, seventh on Birdstone in 2004, and fifteenth on Sun King in 2005. When reporters asked me about not having won a Derby, as if I were somehow jinxed and couldn't sleep because of it, I said I was fine with it. Many great jockeys had never won a Derby, so I didn't see it as something I had to attain for my career to be complete. If it wasn't meant to be, it wasn't meant to be. Coming from where I had, I knew there were worse things in life.

Of course, I also couldn't have come this far without having a strong competitive streak. Nothing keeps me going more than the thrill of winning, or even better, the sensation of being three-quarters of the way through a race and knowing you're in position to win. I badly wanted to experience that at Churchill Downs on the first Saturday in May, and I remained optimistic that I eventually would.

As the days dwindled leading up to the Derby, Bob Frieze noticed my optimism.

"Boy, I know he's a good horse, but you're really feeling good about him, aren't you?" he said one day on the phone.

"Yes," I said, "I'm feeling very, very good."

I felt even better after Barbaro's final pre-Derby work at Churchill Downs, exactly one week before the race. He went out early on a foggy Saturday, two days after having been shipped over from Keeneland. Michael decided it was time to push him a little, give him one faster workout to get him used to running hard and hopefully sharpen him for the Derby.

Peter took him out and jogged him to get him ready, but just as the work was about to start, another horse running near them threw its rider. Sirens sounded, signaling a loose horse on the track. Peter had to pull up. He circled the track, loosened Barbaro up again, and took off a second time.

Peter never asks a horse for much, Michael told me later, but he asked Barbaro for just a little more as they came through the stretch, and Barbaro responded brilliantly, roaring to the finish line with his eyes wide and his legs pumping. Michael watched on horseback from a corner of the track and then rode over to meet Peter. Normally calmer than the calmest sea, Peter was wide-eyed himself, breathless and exhilarated.

"This is the Derby winner!" Peter exclaimed, still sitting on top of the horse. "Michael, no one is going to beat that."

Barbaro had covered a half mile in forty-six seconds, two seconds faster than most horses and easily faster than any Derby contender had worked that week. As Michael led Barbaro back to his barn, Michael's cell phone started ringing like crazy. Clockers—track employees who timed morning works—and several veteran horsemen who had been watching wanted Michael to know they hadn't seen a horse work that impressively in four or five years.

Some might wonder if a horse had wasted his best effort by working that fast a week before a race, but no one thought that now. They thought the opposite was true—Barbaro was in such prime condition that he couldn't help going that fast.

I wasn't at the track to see the work because I rode at Aqueduct that day. But TVG, the racing TV network, showed video of the Derby contenders' latest works, and I stopped to watch Barbaro's on a TV in the jockeys' room in New York that afternoon.

"My God," I thought as I watched.

I had never seen a horse look stronger or more eager. He all but ate up the ground as he came through the stretch. I thought of all the second-guessing Michael had endured. So he didn't know what he was doing? What a joke! Michael had taken a talented horse and, mostly out of the public's view, polished that talent until it dazzled. Unlike Harlan's Holiday, Barbaro was building to a peak, not coming down. He was fresh and fit, and after months of training, had figured out how to run on dirt. Instead of digging with his front legs, he had mastered the gliding action he used on grass.

I was a happy man as I went out to ride at Aqueduct. That night, I called Liliana in Florida and told her to make plans to bring Louis to Louisville for the Derby along with Patty. Louis was just eleven and had never been to the Derby, but if I wanted him and the rest of my family to be there when I won the darn race, I needed to act now. I might never have a better chance.

The Derby post position draw was held on Wednesday, May 3, in Louisville. At the start, a horse's name was selected randomly, and its connections then had a minute to decide which starting post they wanted. They could choose any post, from 1 to 20. Then another horse's name was selected and its connections had a minute to pick any of the remaining posts. The goal was not to end up with a post on the extreme outside or extreme inside. Few Derby winners came from there.

Michael and I discussed strategy before the draw, which I watched on ESPN. He was the trainer, but in this case, he wanted what I wanted. He obviously didn't know when his chance to pick would come, but we went through various possibilities.

"What if our choice is somewhat inside or somewhat outside? What do you want then?" he asked.

That was a tough call. Ordinarily you want to be closer to the rail because then you're closer to where you want to end up and don't have to run as far, but in a twenty-horse field, some people like to be outside because there's so much traffic inside and they don't want to get caught in that.

"Take the inside," I told Michael.

"Really? Are you sure?" Michael asked.

"I'm sure," I said. "He's a good horse, a very good horse. I'm going to ride him like a good horse. I'm confident. If you say he can take dirt in the face, I don't have any doubts about being inside. We'll be fine."

When our time to pick came, in about the middle of the draw, Michael immediately called me on my cell.

"As I see it, we can have the number eight or number thirteen post. Which do you like?" he asked.

"Take the eight," I said.

I was happy with that. It wasn't the far outside or far inside, and we were sandwiched between Sharp Humor, our speedy rival from Florida, and Bob and John, a colt that liked the lead. Both would break ahead of Barbaro, giving him targets to chase right away. He would want to follow them, and that would help me get his attention and get him into the race.

Some of the other top contenders didn't fare as well with their draws. Lawyer Ron and Brother Derek got stuck with posts 17 and 18. Bob and John would come out of No. 4. We were much more fortunate. My idea of a perfect trip around the oval was becoming a real possibility. Coming out of the No. 8 hole, I could hopefully put Barbaro just off the lead for a mile and then turn him loose in the stretch.

If I avoided early traffic trouble and that scenario developed, the other nineteen horses didn't have a chance. I could hardly wait

CHAPTER 8

The Ride of a Lifetime

L iliana, Patty, and Louis met me in Louisville on the Friday before the Derby. They flew in from Florida, I flew in from New York, and we met at our hotel near Churchill Downs. That night Liliana and I attended the Mint Jubilee Gala, an annual black-tie affair benefiting cancer research. More than 1,400 people were there, and Derby jockeys dominated the spotlight. We walked a Hollywood-style red carpet on our way in, stopping to give interviews, and were introduced individually to big applause.

There were Derby Eve parties all over town, limousines crisscrossing on the streets, the city overflowing with racing fans, high rollers, pro athletes, politicians, and movie stars. Anticipation hung in the air like a low-flying cloud. More than 150,000 people would cram into Churchill Downs to watch the Derby the next day.

It is hard to believe the Derby hadn't always been America's biggest race, but actually, it was first run in 1875 and didn't become a national spectacle until the 1930s. Kentucky has always been a horse-breeding center, but its racetracks had financial troubles that kept the Derby from flowering. A turn-of-the-century Louisville businessman, Matt Winn, single-handedly grew it by putting it on radio and television, bringing in celebrities and New York sportswriters, and making it seem important to people everywhere. By the 1950s it was racing's premier event, a springtime fixture on the national sports calendar, as anticipated as the World Series of baseball in the fall.

Unfortunately, horse racing fell into a decline as pro football and other sports surpassed it in popularity in the 1960s and '70s, but the Derby was such a landmark event that it never lost its audience. In fact, it was bigger and better than ever in 2006, with massive crowds and large TV audiences. Any sport that wants attention today has to stage a popular annual event like the Super Bowl, and while racing struggles the rest of the year, it is still the major leagues on the first Saturday in May.

Liliana and I didn't stay late at the Mint Jubilee because the next day's racing card started at 11:00 a.m., so I had to be up early. As my head hit the pillow, I dared to think that the next day might bring my greatest victory ever. I tried not to let my emotions overtake me. My mother surely would have been with us if her health hadn't declined. I missed her terribly, never more than now. But I was riding a wonderful horse with a great chance to win the Derby, and I knew she would be proud.

I awoke early the next morning, went downstairs with Liliana, and ate my usual breakfast—a piece of toast with a dash of jam on it, and a cup of coffee. Save for a few snacks, that was all I would eat until dinner, after the Derby.

Our hotel was crammed with racing fans, and many of them recognized me and wished me luck. As I went back to my room to get ready, Barbaro was taking a brisk jog on the track at Churchill Downs. Michael had wanted him to get out of the barn and shake his legs, but he hooked up with another horse and ran a fairly competitive half mile before Peter finally collared him. Some trainers would have been horrified to have their horse go so fast a few hours before a race, but it seems Barbaro was so primed to go that he couldn't help himself. Michael and Peter expected him to run the same way that afternoon. Peter, in fact, was so confident he told me later he would have been shocked if a horse other than Barbaro won the Derby. In the public's eyes, he was just one of the leading contenders, but to Michael and Peter—and to me, too—he was far and away the best, clearly superior.

Liliana drove me to Churchill Downs in our rental car and dropped me off at 8:30 a.m. I needed to get settled and ready for a long day—I had mounts in seven races, including the Derby—and didn't want to get stuck in the traffic jam that would soon swarm the track. I went to the jockeys' room, greeted my valet, sat in the sauna a while to sweat off a few pounds, took a shower, and checked the papers. Other jockeys started filing in. I was lockering in a corner with Cornelio Velasquez, a good friend from Panama; Corey Nakatani, a California-based veteran who had won almost 3,000 races; and two young Panamanians, Fernando Jara and Eddie

Castro. We looked forward to having a fun day together, sharing some laughs to break the tension, and maybe throwing a few elbows when we were on the track. It was an unwritten rule that we wouldn't talk about our Derby mounts. That was bad luck and bad form.

At 11:00 a.m., we started racing before a sparse crowd, but with the weather sunny and warm, the stands and infield rapidly filled until almost 160,000 people were present. The day's first graded stakes race was a 7½-furlong sprint for three-year-old fillies, run in the early afternoon. I was on a 7–1 shot. We sat on the rail, inside of the favorite, and I asked her to run turning for home. She pulled away to win. I hoped it was an omen.

As long as the day was, I didn't have a chance to see Barbaro. He and the other Derby horses were in their barns on the other side of the grounds, and I was too busy getting on and off horses to get in a visit. I was thinking about him all day, though, and called Michael just to touch base and see what was up. He told me about Barbaro's brisk jog earlier that morning, which made me more excited.

Finally, the sun began to slide toward the western horizon, and it was time for the Derby. I hadn't been nervous all day, this being my seventh Derby, but I began to feel butterflies as post time approached. Mostly, I was confident—not overconfident, just certain of what Barbaro could do. I had watched him develop through the winter and spring, dating back to my first glimpse of him at the Laurel Futurity. He had come a long way, and in my mind, there was no stopping him now.

The jockeys' room fell quiet after an afternoon of bantering. In our corner, we sat and watched NBC's Derby telecast, which started more than an hour before the race. It featured up-close profiles of several trainers and jockeys, including Michael. Between his Olympic career and the story of him rescuing three young children from a burning plane crash, he had quite a personal history. He had stayed in touch with the three children he saved, who were now in their twenties. They were in Louisville to see him run a horse in the Derby for the first time. What a story that would be if Barbaro won.

My valet gave me the Jacksons' silks, and I slipped them on along with a clean helmet and four pairs of goggles. Before I went down to the open-air paddock, I watched on TV as the horses were walked from their barns on the backside around to the grandstand, where they would be saddled in the paddock. It was quite a promenade—the horses and their trainers and owners walked clockwise around the first turn of the track, hugging the outer rail, as thousands of fans screamed their names.

Jose, Barbaro's groom, led him on his walk, with Michael and Peter and their families close behind. An NBC reporter walked alongside Michael and asked him some questions, which he answered with a big smile on his face, like he knew something great was about to happen. Just before I left for the paddock, I saw on TV that Barbaro was acting up again, kicking at Michael as he had before the Florida Derby. Thankfully, he didn't land any blows this time.

By the time I got to the paddock, Barbaro had been saddled and suddenly was all business, ready to go. I got in his face and greeted him, making eye contact. The Derby paddock was a madhouse, a scene guaranteed to upset a nervous horse, with swarms of people walking around inside the rail, and thousands of fans hovering. But Barbaro calmly took it all in and didn't flinch.

I spoke to the Jacksons, who told me another three-year-old they had bred, a colt named George Washington, had won a major race in England, the Two Thousand Guineas, about eight hours earlier. Unlike Barbaro, they had parted ways with George Washington, selling him as a yearling for more than $2 million in 2004. But it was still quite an achievement to breed the winner of a race that dated to the early 1800s. Hopefully, that was an omen, too.

Of course, I also spoke to Michael and Peter. Michael didn't have much to say. His job was over. He had gotten the horse to the Derby, doing it his way. He shook my hand and wished me luck.

"Let's go out and win our first Kentucky Derby, Edgar," he said with a smile.

Peter said, "Ride him with confidence, Edgar. You know what kind of horse he is. He has been through it all, raced on the inside and on the outside, learned how to rate [sit behind other horses early in a race] and take dirt in the face. He can do anything."

Peter gave me a leg up onto Barbaro, and I led my big guy out to the track for the post parade, patting him on the side and holding a one-way conversation to let him know I was there: "You're a good boy. Are you ready to run? I know you are."

He was completely relaxed. Having seen tapes of champions such as Secretariat, Seattle Slew, and Affirmed, I knew they came out to race with obvious confidence, almost an attitude, like a powerful heavyweight jumping into a boxing ring before a fight. They held their heads up, walked with purpose, and looked the other horses in the eyes. Barbaro did all that. He walked and jogged with his head bobbing up and down, looking straight ahead. Behind us, Sharp Humor hung his head low, like he knew he was about to get beat.

The betting public had gone back and forth all day, unable to decide on a clear-cut favorite. They liked Barbaro, Brother Derek, and Sweetnorthernsaint about the same, meaning none would go off as a short-odds favorite. Sweetnorthernsaint finally surged ahead in the minutes just before post time. He would go off as the favorite at 11–2, followed by Barbaro at 6–1, Brother Derek at 8–1, and Sinister Minister at 10–1.

Loading fourteen horses into the main starting gate and six more into an outer auxiliary gate was a tedious process that took three or four minutes, testing the patience of the first horses that went in. Barbaro had a bit of a wait after going into the No. 8 hole, but he stood quietly, a pro all the way. I kept murmuring to him, reassuring him that I was there and we were in this together. Finally, all twenty horses were in. There was a brief pause, a moment of silence and anticipation, and then the gate opened.

Barbaro, incredibly, stumbled taking his first step and pitched forward coming out of the gate.

An average horse might have fallen, dumped me, or taken

so long to start running that he couldn't possibly have caught up. But Barbaro wasn't an average horse. He gathered himself, regained his balance, and took off. The bobble didn't faze him. Within three strides he was in hot pursuit of fast-starting Sharp Humor, running just ahead of us.

As the field charged through the front stretch and headed for the first turn, Barbaro settled into a nice running rhythm with his left leg leading. We were three or four lengths wide of the rail, and three or four lengths behind the frontrunners, Sinister Minister and Keyed Entry. Sinister Minister only knew one way to go, all out; I had known he was going to be there. And I certainly knew Keyed Entry. Neither would last, I thought.

My goal was to find some running room, a place where Barbaro could relax, a few lengths off the lead. It happened easily—effortlessly, really. I guided him to the spot, and no one else was there. He relaxed and galloped along nicely and easily, not at all upset to see a couple of horses ahead of him. As we went around the first turn, I was exactly where I wanted to be. If someone moved to pass us, I was going to let them go. Barbaro was barely exerting himself.

Coming out of the first turn and straightening into the backstretch, he switched to his right lead, just as he was supposed to do. The three horses ahead of us were all to our inside, so after all of my concern, there was no dirt hitting Barbaro in the face. He couldn't have been in a better position, especially knowing the speed in front of us wouldn't last.

As we reached the half-mile mark, I wanted to see if he was on his game, so I chirped once. He immediately started to run harder. Amazing! Amid all that noise and excitement, he was totally focused, just waiting for a signal, and he knew not to go until the signal came. But I wanted to save his best for later, so I pulled him back in and kept him under wraps. He seemed fine with that. We kept rolling along.

Before we reached the far turn I quickly looked back and to the inside to see if someone was making a move. I knew Barbaro was ready to go, and I felt like it was time, but I didn't want to move yet if no one was pressuring us.

No one was approaching. I sat still, avoiding giving the horse any signal.

A few moments later I looked back again because I thought the time was right. This time, Sweetnorthernsaint and a 26–1 shot named Showing Up were charging at us from the inside. Sweetnorthernsaint pulled even, and Showing Up actually passed us and moved ahead. I didn't panic. I knew Barbaro would accelerate with force when I asked. I didn't mind letting those horses go ahead. They gave him a target to chase.

He started accelerating on his own as we made our way around the far turn. I didn't whip him, show him the whip, or even chirp at him. He just lowered his head and took off. He had waited long enough and instinctively knew when to move.

Keyed Entry and Sinister Minister had ruled the race for a mile, but as Barbaro accelerated, they fell away as if they were walking rather than running. Sweetnorthernsaint also fell away. His backers had picked the wrong contender.

In just a few strides, near the end of the second turn, Barbaro zoomed from fourth place into the lead.

When I tell people what happened next, they don't believe

me. But it did happen: when Barbaro made the lead in the Kentucky Derby, his ears shot up straight like a rabbit's, and he stalled. Looking back, you can see he was startled. He had been running hard and focusing on the horses in front of him, and suddenly, they were gone. His reaction was, "Whoa, where'd everyone go?"

When he paused, I took out the stick, showed it to him, and chirped at him. It was really time to go. And he was with me all the way. His ears came back down and he took off with a whooosh. I never hit him because I didn't have to hit him. The sensation was unlike any I had ever felt on a horse. It was like being in a car going from zero to sixty in a matter of seconds. This was his old burst of acceleration, the one he had on the turf months earlier. He had needed a couple of races on dirt to make the transition, but he had figured out what he needed to do. He knew how to run on the dirt now, and oh, my God, did he run.

He pulled in front at the top of the stretch, and I showed him the stick again, then just let him go. He surged ahead by two lengths, then three. When I looked back with an eighth of a mile to go, no one was coming. Nineteen horses were stretched out behind us, in various states of exhaustion and depression. They were finished. The only question now was, how much would we win by?

I thought back to that spectacular video of his last pre-Derby work. He was moving the same way, gobbling up huge amounts of ground with every stride, excited just to be going at top speed. He reached farther and farther out with his front legs, showing a worldwide television audience what he could do.

The lead grew to four lengths, five. I showed him the stick once more at the sixteenth pole and then put it away for good. He was ahead by five lengths, six, no challenge in sight, the great crowd roaring. I experienced a moment of pure joy as we approached the finish line. The boy from Peru was going to win the greatest race in the world. A super horse had delivered me to the doorstep of history.

We were six and a half lengths ahead of a 30–1 shot named Bluegrass Cat at the wire, while most of the rest of the field was ten to twenty lengths back. All those other horses with supposedly legitimate Derby credentials? Barbaro had demolished them.

When I loosened my hold after we crossed the finish line, he eased up and looked around, as if to say, "That's it? I have to stop?" He had just run away with the Kentucky Derby, but he wanted to keep going. If this wasn't a horse ready for the mile-and-a-half Belmont Stakes, there would never be one.

As we slowed down and I began to focus on what had just happened, tears flooded my eyes. I thought of my mother, who had wanted to see me win the Kentucky Derby but missed it by four months. I was thrilled that Liliana, Patty, and Louis were in the crowd, but devastated that my mother wasn't with them.

The first person to speak to me was Cornelio Velasquez, one of my closest friends. He had just finished sixth on Showing Up and jogged by on his horse.

"*Felicito! Felicito!*" he shouted with a smile.

Congratulations!

I smiled and shouted my thanks. Then Ramon Dominguez,

who had finished second on Bluegrass Cat, also rode by and shouted congratulations.

As Barbaro stopped, a broadcaster and former jockey, Donna Brothers, pulled alongside me on her horse. She was an old friend from when we rode against each other in Boston, and she now worked for NBC. Her job on Derby Day was to ride out with a microphone and interview the winning jockey as soon as the race ended.

It was just the two of us out on the track, but I knew an international TV audience was watching.

"Edgar, congratulations on your first Kentucky Derby win," Donna said. "It was so impressive on Barbaro's part. What kind of horse is this, and how does it feel to get your first win?"

I couldn't help it: I still had my mother on my mind. "First of all, Mom, I hope you're listening," I said, feeling out of breath. "This is for you."

My voice started to crack. Donna stepped in and told the audience about my mother passing away in January, and said, "I'm sure she was up there rooting for you to win."

As she spoke, I told myself to get it together. I did not want to cry on national TV. And besides, this was about Barbaro, not me.

"Barbaro is a very excellent horse," I said. "He has just shown what kind of quality horse he is. I was very confident today. He proved he can run. I'm very happy."

Donna asked about this being my seventh attempt to win the Derby.

"I was very, very confident today. In America, dreams come true," I said.

As I spoke, Barbaro nibbled playfully at Donna's pony. He didn't seem the least bit tired. I wondered if anyone else noticed he was barely breathing hard.

I steered him clockwise, back toward the finish line and the winner's circle, helped by an outrider who picked us up and guided us. As we passed the grandstand, we were greeted by a huge, roaring ovation, tens of thousands of people cheering and calling out Barbaro's name. Kentucky racing fans are as knowledgeable as any, and they knew they had just seen greatness.

I just pointed to Barbaro. I wanted the people to know that I felt he had done the work. He was the champion. I was just along for the ride.

As the crowd roared, I reached down, patted Barbaro, and played with his ears. He pranced for a couple of steps. "You're the big man now," I said to him. "You're the king."

I reached the winner's circle and handed Barbaro to Jose. Michael was there; I leapt off the horse, and Michael wrapped me in a huge embrace, practically lifting me off the ground.

"That was perfect, just so perfect," he said. He seemed almost speechless.

Then Peter hugged me, pulled back, smiled, and nodded his head. He had expected that to happen. "Here," he said as he handed over a bottle of water. The ex-jockey knew I needed it.

The next hugs—and best of all—came from Liliana, Patty, and Louis. They had come from the stands and run across the track to join the celebration. They smothered me with kisses and exclamations.

"We're so proud of you, Daddy!" Patty shouted.

Liliana just smiled and shook her head. She didn't need to speak to let me know how happy she was.

The feeling of winning the Derby was even greater than I had expected because of Barbaro's picture-perfect performance. Even in the winner's circle, he was still a strong-willed character. When Michael tried to put Churchill Downs's famed garland of roses on him, he shrugged them off, wanting no part of them. Then he stood tall and still, like the gentleman he was, through the winner's circle ceremony as the Kentucky governor spoke and interviewers questioned Roy Jackson, Michael, and me.

"He's a super horse," I told the TV audience. "Hopefully we can get the Triple Crown."

After the ceremony, Barbaro left for the barn with Jose and Peter. His reward would be a huge dinner and the chance to relax. He had earned whatever he had coming. I hugged his neck as he departed. "I'm so proud of you, fella," I said softly.

The next few hours were a whirlwind of activity, starting with the press conference for the winning horse's "team." Liliana, Patty, and Louis sat right beside me on the dais as reporters asked about Barbaro and the race and also about my long journey from Peru. It began to sink in that I had won the Kentucky Derby.

One reporter asked about me being so exuberant on the horse right after the race, when I raised my hands over my head like a triumphant boxer and pointed to Barbaro.

"You normally don't show emotion," the reporter said.

I agreed that, win or lose, I usually was straight-faced after a race. But I had never experienced anything like Barbaro's sprint in the final quarter mile.

"I got caught up in the moment," I said. "I wanted people to know what I thought about this horse."

After the press conference I did individual interviews with a bunch of radio and TV reporters. My cell phone rang nonstop. Edgar Jr. called from Daytona, crying with joy.

I gave interviews for more than an hour, and then finally was free to go back to the jockeys' room. My friends and rivals broke into applause when they saw me. I signed their programs, answered questions from more reporters, took a few more calls, and finally showered and put on a coat and tie. A track official took me to a postrace reception at the Kentucky Derby Museum, attached to the grandstand. It was crawling with people, and I was swarmed by well-wishers. Someone asked if Barbaro could fly. The race was being replayed over and over on a TV screen so large it took up an entire wall.

Suddenly, I was starving. I had barely eaten since breakfast that morning. I asked a waiter to bring me food, anything, and he brought crackers and cheese. The reception was for drinks, not dinner. I was afraid to drink, having eaten so little. Liliana, the kids, and I finally made our break at around nine. The kids were exhausted. We dropped them at the hotel and set out to find a place to eat, but we hadn't planned ahead and made reservations anywhere.

Then Rick Dutrow, one of my best friends in racing, called my cell. He was a New York–based trainer who used me on all of his horses—a major client. He didn't have a Derby horse, but he came to Louisville every year and hosted a post-Derby party at his hotel near the airport.

"What are you doing?" he shouted.

"Looking for something to eat, actually," I said.

He didn't have food at the party, just drinks and music, but he said he would fix me up. Liliana and I went over to his hotel, and he fed us delicious steaks and fries. I relaxed, signed some autographs, and sat back. What a day, I thought to myself.

We went back to the hotel at around eleven, because we had to get up early the next day. I was flying back to New York to ride, and Liliana and the kids were flying back to South Florida out of Cincinnati, some seventy-five miles away.

The night before, when my head hit the pillow, I had thought this might be a momentous day for me. Now, hitting the same pillow twenty-four hours later, I couldn't help but take stock. I thought back to all the hardships I had endured—the days when I couldn't get mounts at Calder, the suspensions at Suffolk Downs. I thought about all the hard work, all the ups and downs. Winning the Kentucky Derby was the ultimate payoff. Nothing could compare to it. So many jockeys went through their whole careers without ever riding in the race, much less winning it, and I had won it. I felt so blessed.

And so grateful to my guy Barbaro.

A Triple Crown Champ?

When a chestnut colt named Sir Barton won the Kentucky Derby, Preakness Stakes, and Belmont Stakes in 1919, he wasn't acclaimed as the first winner of horse racing's Triple Crown. The phrase wasn't even coined until 1930, when *Daily Racing Form* columnist Charles Hatton used it to describe another sweep of the three races—this time by a colt named Gallant Fox. Hatton's term established the springtime races as a single mountain that horsemen should attempt to climb with their best three-year-olds. The public bought into it, and a tradition was born.

In the beginning, the feat was viewed as challenging but not impossible. Six times in the first eighteen years after Hatton coined the phrase, a single horse won the 1¼-mile Kentucky Derby, went to Pimlico Race Course in Baltimore, Maryland, and won the Preakness at 1³/₁₆ miles, and then moved on to New York to capture the 1½-mile Belmont Stakes, a race nicknamed the "Test of Champions" because of its grueling distance.

But after Citation became the eighth Triple Crown winner in 1948, horses suddenly had a much harder time winning all three. In fact, there was a quarter-century draught until Secretariat won in 1973, and then, after Seattle Slew and Affirmed went back-to-back in 1977 and 1978, a complete blackout. By the time Barbaro won at Churchill Downs in 2006, it had been twenty-eight years since the Derby winner had gone on to win the Preakness and Belmont. There had been ten close calls in that span, as horses such as Silver Charm and Smarty Jones teased the public by winning the first two races before losing in the Belmont—I played a role in two of the near-misses—but no Triple Crown winner.

Sports fans badly wanted to see a Triple Crown victory, and almost from the moment Barbaro won the Derby, he was seen by many experts as the best candidate in years. He was just the sixth horse in history to come out of the Derby undefeated, and his margin of victory was the Derby's largest since Assault, a Triple Crown winner, won by eight lengths in 1946.

Bob Baffert, the trainer of three previous Derby winners, called Barbaro "awesome" after the race. D. Wayne Lukas, the trainer of four Derby winners, said he probably wouldn't even bother to enter a horse in the Preakness, run two weeks after the Derby. "Barbaro is pretty dominant. It's a little more than I need right now," Lukas said.

After watching his horse Jazil finish a distant fourth to Barbaro in the Derby, trainer Kiaran McLaughlin said, "He's a very good horse, a future star, or maybe a 'now' star. Because of his pedigree and the way he trains, works, and runs, a mile and a half [in the Belmont] is not a problem for him.

He might even like it more than a mile and a quarter. Winning the Triple Crown is a tough thing to do, but it seems well within his grasp."

I had to agree. I had always known he was talented—remember, I had him winning the English Derby after our first race together—but after the Derby I reassessed. When I was asked about him on national television in the winner's circle, I said, "He's a super horse. Hopefully we can get the Triple Crown." I knew saying that would increase the pressure on us—me, Michael, and most of all, Barbaro—to do it. Millions of people would think it was a realistic goal, and in some cases, expect no less. But I believed in him. If I had won the Derby narrowly, whipping and driving him through the stretch, I would have said, "OK, he's very good, but he had to go all out." But Barbaro won by a huge margin without me even touching him! And dirt wasn't even his favorite racing surface! Now he had me wondering: Just what kind of horse was he? The one we had dreamed about? The one we had hoped for? It sure looked like it.

It seemed many people were thinking along the same lines. On the morning after the Derby, as I flew from Louisville back to New York, I could hardly take a step without people breaking out in applause, stopping to congratulate me, and saying they would be rooting for Barbaro to win a Triple Crown. Many of the messages on my jammed cell-phone voice mail were from friends saying they would be rooting for Barbaro to make history. I guess when you're undefeated and win the Derby by six and a half lengths, you cause people to think big.

The two weeks between the Derby and Preakness were a blur. I was in New York, riding at Aqueduct, and trying to concentrate on each horse I got on, but Barbaro and the Triple Crown were never far from the front of my mind. Friends and family members kept calling to say how happy they were for me. Fans shouted congratulations and wished me the best every time I got on a horse. I fielded what seemed like a thousand media requests and said yes to them all. Photographers came to my house and took pictures for magazine stories. I did radio interviews in Peru, Argentina, and Chile, appeared on the *Cold Pizza* morning show on ESPN, and did a live interview on MSNBC. It was overwhelming. No matter where I was, I always had to be somewhere else soon. A public relations pro whom I knew from the racetrack stepped in and helped me organize everything and get from place to place.

The highlight, no question, was getting to throw out the first pitch before a New York Yankees game at Yankee Stadium. Although I'm so busy I don't have time to closely follow baseball, I keep an eye on the Yankees from a distance, and I knew then-Yankee manager Joe Torre, who is a big racing fan, comes to the track, and owns horses, several of which I had ridden. I had also attended his "Safe at Home" charity auction, which raised money to fight domestic violence.

I went to the stadium on May 11, five days after the Derby, and met up with Joe several hours before the game. He took me down to the locker room and introduced me around. The players were great. We shook hands and they congratulated me on the Derby. A few even wanted autographs. Bobby Frankel, the horse trainer, was also there—he trains some of Joe's horses—and suggested I practice throwing so I wouldn't embarrass myself in front of the crowd. That was a good idea. I had played soccer and a little volleyball as a boy, but no baseball.

Joe grabbed some guy in uniform (I wasn't sure who it was) and sent us out to throw on the field, in foul territory. We started near each other and stepped farther and farther back every few throws. Bobby Frankel and Bob Frieze, who had also come with me, were jokingly betting whether I would throw the ball on the fly all the way from the pitcher's mound to the catcher at home plate, or come up short and bounce the ball in the dirt. My practice throws were mostly good. After a few minutes, the guy in uniform said, "He's fine. He throws like a pro."

Having won the Derby in front of 157,000 people (and who knows how many more on TV) a few days earlier, I wasn't nervous about performing before 50,000 at Yankee Stadium. The public address announcer introduced me, and there was a roar. I waved as I walked out to the mound. A replay of the finish of the Derby showed on the big-screen scoreboard, with Barbaro pulling away. I turned to the catcher, wound up, and threw . . . a strike! I couldn't wipe the smile off my face as I left the field and took a seat in the stands to watch the game.

I was having a good time as the jockey of the Derby winner, but I wasn't running around making appearances and giving interviews just because I wanted to be famous or see myself on TV. I was doing it for my sport. Racing had been in the shadows for a long time and needed a new hero to attract attention. I was thinking Barbaro could be that hero. Everywhere I went, people asked if he was as special as he looked, and whether he could win the Triple Crown. I thought it was a great chance to bring more people to racing and hopefully generate something positive on a large scale.

It was quite a coincidence that I was now gunning for a Triple Crown on a horse with such a big chance. I had played a part in ruining the Triple Crown bids of two other horses. A few writers had even called me "the Triple Crown killer"—not my favorite nickname, although I was proud of what I had done.

The first bid was War Emblem's in 2002. He was a speedy colt that swept through the Derby and Preakness and came to the Belmont as a big favorite. He stumbled badly out of the gate, but his jockey, Victor Espinoza, got him going, and he rallied to take the lead after a mile. But he had used too much of himself overcoming the start, had nothing left, and faded. Meanwhile, I was on a 71–1 shot named Sarava. I had raced a few lengths off the lead, saving ground, and then asked him to go in the stretch. Sarava put his nose in front of a first-rate horse named Medaglia d'Oro and kept it there, winning by half a length.

Fans had wanted War Emblem to win and were disappointed about Sarava's victory, but I didn't feel I had stopped the Triple Crown. War Emblem basically beat himself with that stumble. After that, someone was going to make the most of the opportunity, and I was thrilled it had been me. This was my first victory in a Triple Crown race, and on the longest shot ever to win the Belmont. Sarava paid $142.50 to win on a $2 bet.

Two years later, Smarty Jones also won the Derby and Preakness and came to New York looking to make history. He was undefeated and wildly popular. There were 120,000 fans at Belmont Park when he went for his Triple Crown. His jockey, Stewart Elliott, was a friend; we had ridden against each other at Suffolk Downs and stayed in touch. He was based in Philadelphia, where my brother Anibal rode, so I was happy to see him win the Derby and Preakness.

Smarty was a 3–10 choice to win the Belmont. I was on a 36–1 shot named Birdstone that had run seventh in the Kentucky Derby while getting bumped all over the place. He was a little horse that ran his guts out, and his trainer, Nick Zito, decided to give him a shot in the Belmont.

When Smarty took the early lead, a horse named Eddington challenged him before falling back, and then another named Rock Hard Ten took a run at him. While they pressed him, I sat back and let Birdstone get comfortable. With a half mile to go, the only horses still running were Smarty and mine. Part of me wanted to hold back. Can you believe that? This was a Triple Crown race with a million-dollar purse, and I didn't want to win? But I had seen fans surround Smarty just to see and touch him, and it had been a long time since people had gotten that excited about a horse. His success would be great for the sport.

When we turned for home, Smarty had a three-length lead, and the fans were going crazy, thinking they were about to witness history. No one saw me coming. But I had a ton of horse left. Every time I asked Birdstone for more, he gave me more.

Sometimes in a race I find myself behind either a young rider or one who is struggling, and I think, "Don't beat him, Edgar. He needs this more than you." But you can't think like that. Victor Sanchez taught me that years ago. You have to be tough. You can't stop riding hard. And I didn't on Birdstone.

As we started closing on Smarty, I thought, No way! This can't be happening! Then I saw Stewart look back and put his stick in front of Smarty at the quarter pole. I knew I had him. Stewart hadn't needed the stick in the Derby or Preakness because Smarty had won easily, but he needed it now because Smarty was running out of gas.

I started to feel good, and at the same time, terrible. I knew I had the race long before the end. I almost stopped whipping Birdstone because Smarty was done. Birdstone passed him in the final furlong and won by a length.

The track went completely silent. I knew everyone wanted Smarty, and part of me did, too. I didn't enjoy beating him. After we passed under the wire, I leaned over to Stewart and shouted, "I'm so sorry."

After stopping those Triple Crowns, I was suddenly on the other side now, trying to win one. I knew from my own experience that most people would be rooting for Barbaro, including some of the trainers and jockeys we were competing against. But they wouldn't let their feelings keep them from trying to beat us. Winning all three races would be a challenge. There was a reason no horse had done it since 1978. But Barbaro was the one to do it. I was convinced. He had the talent. He had the breeding. He was in a terrific trainer's hands.

Immediately after the Derby he was shipped to Fair Hill, Michael's base, where his life was 180 degrees different than it was at any racetrack. Fair Hill was a huge wooded park in Cecil County, Maryland, a peaceful place set back from major roads. The training track was a half mile from Michael's barn and had a synthetic surface that was easy on horses. Barbaro loved it. Every morning he walked from the barn to the track, exercised under Peter, and walked back. Then, because of all the open space, Michael turned him out in a fenced-in pen, and he ran around and rolled in the dirt. He loved being outside. Horses stabled at racetracks spent maybe an hour outside every day, but Barbaro enjoyed long stretches of time outside at Fair Hill.

I called Michael to check on the horse and ask if I could ride him when he worked (thanks but no thanks). Michael's report was 100 percent positive: Barbaro was happy, hungry, and seemingly unfazed by the Derby. He was enjoying the sunshine, preparing for the Preakness, and receiving a ton of attention. The national media was crawling all over the barn, and Michael was walking around with a big smile, having proved wrong those who questioned him for giving Barbaro just one race in the thirteen weeks before the Derby. Now that the horse had won the Derby, Michael looked like a maverick genius. Barbaro had all sorts of energy left for the rest of the Triple Crown.

Because Fair Hill was so close to Baltimore and New York, the horse would be able to spend most of the rest of the Triple Crown season there. The plan was to take him to Pimlico (sixty miles away) a couple of days before the Preakness and then bring him right back after the race. He could follow the same blueprint during the three weeks leading up to the Belmont—spend all but the last few days at Fair Hill before going to New York. He would be relaxed and happy going into both races—primed to perform.

He was so happy at Fair Hill that, in the end, Michael waited as long as possible before sending him to Baltimore. Barbaro arrived at Pimlico on Friday, May 18, some thirty hours before the start of the Preakness. He was installed in stall 40 of the stakes barn, the same stall the Derby winner gets every year.

The Preakness was first run in 1873, making it the oldest of the Triple Crown events, beating the Derby by two years. The race has quite a history, having been won not just by the eleven Triple Crown winners, but also by legendary horses such as Man O' War and Native Dancer. It was a Maryland springtime staple, drawing a huge crowd every year, including tens of thousands of young folks who spent all day partying in the infield.

Racing in Maryland had slumped recently because nearby Delaware and West Virginia had approved slot-machine gambling at their tracks, bringing in revenue that had raised purse levels and attracted better horses, while Maryland's politicians had not approved "slots," leaving its tracks struggling to compete. The situation was dire enough that I had even heard talk of the Preakness being moved, which I doubted would happen and hoped never to see. The Triple Crown had a historic foundation and a familiar routine—after the dizzy high of Louisville, you regrouped two weeks later for another big bang, this time in Baltimore, with everyone chasing the Derby winner.

You could always tell from the size of the Preakness field whether other horsemen respected the Derby winner—an impressive winner translated into fewer Preakness entrants because no one felt it was worthwhile to take him on, while a long-shot Derby winner led to a larger Preakness field because everyone thought they could beat him. Eight other horses had been entered to run against Barbaro, giving the Preakness its smallest field in six years. Barbaro had scared off a lot of people. Only two of the nineteen horses that ran against him in the Derby (Brother Derek and Sweetnorthernsaint) were back for more. Of the non-Derby horses in the field, only one looked dangerous—Bernardini, the green-but-gifted colt I had ridden in March at Gulfstream. He was legitimate, and so were Sweetnorthernsaint and Brother Derek, but I still felt that Barbaro was in another class.

While Barbaro traveled from Fair Hill to Pimlico and settled in, I raced in New York through Friday afternoon, caught an early-evening plane to Baltimore, rented a car, and drove to my brother Javier's house in Woodstock, Maryland, a few miles west of downtown Baltimore. Liliana, Patty, and Louis were already there, having flown up from Florida earlier in the day. We would spend the weekend with Javier and his wife and kids. My family wasn't about to miss this. Patty and Louis had been born in Maryland, and Liliana and I had lived there for almost a decade. It would always feel like home. And now I was coming back as the jockey of the Kentucky Derby winner.

That night we had a mini family reunion. My brother Jorge, who also lived in Maryland, came over with his family. We ate dinner and sat around talking and laughing as the kids played outside. It was a warm, wonderful night, and the house was filled with great expectations. Everyone thought Barbaro would repeat his victory the next day.

And if nothing had gone wrong, he would have.

CHAPTER 10

"I'm Sorry, Just So Sorry"

Saturday dawned clear and warm, with bright sunshine flooding into Javier's house. I awoke early, needing to get to Pimlico before traffic backed up around the track. I had toast and coffee, kissed Liliana good-bye, and headed out in the rental car.

I took the back roads to the track, a familiar commute from my days living and riding in Maryland. As I drove, I thought about my time here. This was where I had established myself as a winner in America. I would always be grateful to the local trainers who used me, the rival jockeys who forced me to ride better, and the stewards who taught me about limits. I had a lot of friends here, and as badly as I wanted to win this Preakness for Barbaro, I also wanted it for them. I had never fared well in Maryland's biggest race, finishing no higher than fourth in eight Preakness starts. The state's racing community would love to see me win, and, I thought, this was certainly the day to do it.

I parked at the track and stopped to see Barbaro on my way to the jockeys' room. I hadn't seen him since the winner's circle in Louisville. He had already been to the track for a morning warm-up jog, which Michael described as "brilliant." He looked ready to run the Preakness now. His muscles bulged, his eyes danced, and he was attentive to noises and people around him. I didn't think he could be doing any better mentally or physically. I stood outside his stall, stroked his neck, and said, "It's going to be a good day, big man." His ears went back. He always loved voices.

I headed on to the jockeys' room on the clubhouse mezzanine, overlooking the finish line. Unlike Churchill Downs, which had recently undergone a makeover, Pimlico creaked with age. But it was spruced up with bright flowers blooming in boxes and pots. Maryland always rose to the occasion for the Preakness.

I greeted my valet and settled in, took a sauna, read the newspapers. The other jockeys started rolling in. Alex Solis was on Brother Derek in the Preakness. Kent Desormeaux, having a Maryland homecoming himself, was on Sweetnorthernsaint. Javier Castellano was on Bernardini. I had a full day of mounts building up to the Preakness. The races started before noon, one going off every forty minutes as the crowd swelled to what was, in the end, the largest in Preakness history—more than 118,000 people. They were in high spirits, anticipating seeing a trained-in-Maryland Derby winner sweep the second jewel of the Triple Crown.

In one of the early races, a sprint, I rode a colt named Songster that outclassed the field and pulled away to win by ten lengths, reminding me of Barbaro in Kentucky. "He did it all by himself," I told a reporter. That's what I had said after the Derby, and I hoped to be able to use the line a third time in a few hours, after the Preakness.

I didn't win any other races on the undercard, but I had a busy afternoon with radio and TV interviews—it seemed everyone wanted to talk to the jockey of the horse gunning for a Triple Crown. I tried to strike the right tone in my answers. I was extremely confident in Barbaro, especially after having seen him that morning—he was like a powerful oak tree rising out of the ground—but I didn't want to come off as cocky. I just said I thought we had a great chance and I hoped our good luck would hold.

Finally, toward the end of a long afternoon of sunshine and noise, post time for the Preakness neared. My valet handed me the Lael Stable silks, and I sat quietly and watched the NBC broadcast. A camera crew stood nearby, and I saw myself on the screen several times. The announcers wanted to build suspense but spoke of Barbaro in the grandest terms, as if there was no doubt he would win.

Barbaro's trip from the barn to the track was much shorter at Pimlico than at Churchill Downs. Jose, Michael, and Peter walked him across the stable area and onto the main track. Then they walked him across the dirt and onto the stretch run of the turf course, where the Preakness horses were saddled, facing the grandstand. Pimlico used an indoor paddock before other races, but saddling the horses on the turf course now enabled the huge crowd to see the Preakness horses.

I met Michael, Peter, and the Jacksons out on the grass.

There wasn't much to do because Michael had already put on Barbaro's saddle while walking him over, a trick that trainers used on horses that gave them trouble in paddocks.

We stood around on the turf course for close to ten minutes while the other horses were saddled. It was unusual for Barbaro to be on the grass before a race. I didn't think anything of it at the time because it didn't seem important, but later, when I looked back and tried to make sense of what happened next, I remembered that change in his routine. Before the Kentucky Derby, Florida Derby, and Holy Bull Stakes, he had been saddled on hard floors of concrete in fully or partially enclosed paddocks. Then he had gone out and run on a hard dirt track. Now he was being saddled on the grass, and I think, horses being creatures of habit, he may have thought he was about to race on grass, which excited him. He was a turf horse at heart, with a turf pedigree. He had started his career with three turf wins. He was never happier than when he was running on grass.

The longer he stood on the grass, the more excited he became. He breathed harder. His muscles tensed. He was noticeably pumped up by the time I got on him, and he was more worked up than usual through the post parade—not nervous but agitated, impatient, a little too eager to get going. Before his prior races he had always been cool and confident, but now he seemed restless, unsettled. He even jumped a couple of times, which he had never done. It was like he could barely wait to run, win, and get back to Fair Hill.

At the time, I just chalked it up to the wild scene around us. The big crowd was making as much noise as Barbaro had ever heard. Rock music was blaring, people were screaming, and the public address announcer was talking nonstop. None of that had bothered him before, but horses can be unpredictable.

At the time, I hoped the change in his behavior was just a minor prerace glitch, and he would run the same once the race started. But then we were loaded into the starting gate, and before it opened, there was a bigger glitch—a disaster.

Barbaro went easily into the No. 6 hole, the back gate clicking shut behind us. With nine horses entered, he waited calmly while the final three were loaded. The last horse to go in was Diabolical, in the No. 9 hole. The colt balked at going in, so Pimlico's gate staff used an old trick to get him loaded. They opened his front starting gate, hoping he wouldn't be as afraid of a more open space. Once he was in, they closed the gate in front of him and quickly also closed the gate behind him.

When Barbaro heard that second click, he suddenly kicked out with his forelegs, opening his front gate on his own. The race hadn't started, but he began to run down the track.

The crowd gasped. A false start is common in sports such as track and swimming, but it is a freak incident in horse racing, a bizarre occurrence. Of the thousands of horses I had sat on in starting gates, only a few had broken though early like this.

It happened in a flash, much too quickly for me to prevent it, but as Barbaro galloped down the track alone, everything seemed to unfold in slow motion. I pulled hard on the reins, telling him not to go. I was horrified. My heart hammered. My mind raced. Why was this happening now, of all times? An outrider (track employee on a horse) came toward us, hoping to help me corral Barbaro and steer him back toward the gate so he could be reloaded and the race could have a proper start. The horse only traveled thirty or forty yards before he came to a halt, but it seemed to take forever.

What had spooked him? Lesser racehorses occasionally break through the gate early because they can't stand to be in an enclosed space any longer and nudge the gate open with their noses. Better racehorses, such as Barbaro, occasionally kick the gate open with their forelegs because of an unusual circumstance, like hearing an extra click and thinking the race is starting.

But whatever caused Barbaro to break through early, he was in trouble now. Horses that break through seldom run well once they're reloaded. For whatever reason, it throws them off their game, and they don't perform.

As Barbaro stopped and I turned him around and directed him back toward the starting gate, I looked down. I was halfway hoping to see blood dripping out of a cut on one of his forelegs. I was halfway hoping I would have to scratch him. The racing world would have been furious, I know—how could I scratch a horse that looked like he was going to win a Triple Crown? But I would have done it without hesitation! Who cared about the Triple Crown? Barbaro had so much ahead of him, so many other races to win. So what if he was scratched now? We could bring him back in three weeks and win the Belmont Stakes in a breeze. Or we could give him a break, switch him back to his original surface, and win the Breeders' Cup Turf or the Arc de Triomphe. He could still make history. Why run him on a day when he suddenly didn't seem quite right?

I was concerned only about his welfare. But in fact, he seemed fine after I maneuvered him back behind the starting gate and paused to examine him before he was reloaded. There was no blood dripping. He wasn't limping. His eyes were bright and alive. He couldn't wait to run. I spoke to Dr. David Zipf, the Pimlico veterinarian, whose job on Preakness day is to stand at the gate and make sure the horses are fine as the race begins. He also carefully examined Barbaro.

"See anything, Doc?" I asked.

"Nothing, Edgar. He looks fine," Dr. Zipf said.

There was no time to communicate with Michael or the Jacksons. They were up in the stands—terribly anxious, for sure. There was no time for them to come down to check on their baby. The other Preakness horses were still in the starting gate, waiting for the race to begin.

It had been less than a minute since Barbaro broke through. I led him back into the gate and spoke to him—"OK, boy, let's do it"—to soothe him and help him get resettled. All I could do was hope for the best.

When the gate opened and all nine horses took off, Barbaro broke fine, right in step with the others. But he wasn't the same. In each of his other races he had broken sharply, powerfully, and quickly found his running rhythm. This time, he seemed dull. He wasn't limping, but it was like he didn't want to run his hardest.

I thought maybe he didn't like the track for some reason, or just needed to settle down. Whatever it was, he was dragging—and I was immediately on alert.

When he made it through the first hundred yards, I hoped

he would get himself established and into the race, but then, suddenly, I felt him weaken, almost as if he had absorbed a punch and been knocked off balance.

I didn't think it was serious at first. I usually know when my horse breaks down underneath me. I've experienced it too often, probably three dozen times in my career. There is a sharp jolt, or the horse veers wildly, or it tumbles and you end up on the ground. In any case, you know the worst has happened. The signs weren't that obvious now. Barbaro just seemed weak, suddenly. I thought maybe he had pulled a muscle.

But whatever was wrong, it was troubling enough to convince me to pull Barbaro up.

Over the years I've developed a personal rule: if I have any concerns about my horse during a race, I stop—either pull up entirely or, if I'm near the finish line, jog lightly to the end. It's not fair to run a horse when you have doubts about his health. I learned my lesson years earlier at Laurel when I got on a 1–5 favorite, the gate opened, and I immediately felt him dragging. I wasn't sure what was wrong, but I kept going all the way around the track even though the horse wasn't himself. We made it to the end, but he didn't come close to winning, and I later found out he had locked his stifle—cramped up—repeatedly. He survived, but I never should have put him through that. Never again, I vowed.

I didn't have set guidelines, just went on gut feeling, instinct. And although I didn't yet think Barbaro was seriously injured, I knew he wasn't right. It was time to act—yes, even with the whole sports world watching.

Here I am *(far left)*, the youngest boy of the eleven kids in my family, with my brother Edwin and my sister Sara in Lima, Peru, 1971. (Courtesy of Jorge Prado)

Sitting on a wall in foggy Boston, shortly after arriving to ride at Suffolk Downs, 1988. (Courtesy of Jorge Prado)

My brother Jorge *(right)* is my pony boy before a race at Suffolk Downs, 1988. (Courtesy of Jorge Prado)

Barbaro prances in the mud during the post parade before the Holy Bull Stakes at Gulfstream Park in Hallandale Beach, Florida, on February 4, 2006. Fortunately, the poor weather conditions didn't bother him. (Eleanor Gustafson/ Horsephotos)

Barbaro races to victory at the Holy Bull Stakes. We were all surprised and delighted by how easily he switched from turf to dirt. (Eleanor Gustafson/Horsephotos)

Barbaro surges ahead of Sharp Humor in the last furlong of the Florida Derby at Gulfstream Park on April 1, 2006. He was a boy at the beginning of the race and a man at the end. (Harold Roth/Horsephotos)

Roy Jackson leads Barbaro and me to the winner's circle after the Florida Derby. I knew then that I would ride him in the Kentucky Derby. (Harold Roth/Horsephotos)

Barbaro runs away from the rest of the field to win the 2006 Kentucky Derby by $6^{1}/_{2}$ lengths, the largest margin of victory since 1946. This race on May 6, 2006, was truly the ride of a lifetime. (Michael J. Marten/Horsephotos)

Barbaro crosses the finish line at the Kentucky Derby. That evening someone asked me if he could fly. I guess the answer was yes. (Horsephotos)

I give Barbaro a congratulatory pat on the neck. He didn't want to stop running. (Horsephotos)

I'm all smiles after the Kentucky Derby. I told the worldwide television audience that dreams come true in America. (Michael J. Marten/Horsephotos)

I acknowledge the crowd's cheers on the way to the winner's circle at Churchill Downs. (Horsephotos)

My daughter, Patty, my wife, Liliana, and my son, Louis, stand beside me during the winner's circle ceremony at Churchill Downs. We were thrilled, but we missed my mother. (Horsephotos)

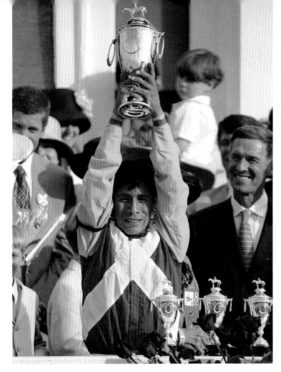

Holding the Kentucky Derby trophy aloft in the winner's circle. This moment made all the hard times worthwhile. (Horsephotos)

Barbaro, with Peter Brette and Michael Matz, at the Fair Hill Training Center in Maryland during the weeks between the Kentucky Derby and the Preakness Stakes. Barbaro loved it there. (Michael J. Marten/Horsephotos)

Barbaro *(right)* teases his next-door neighbor in the stakes barn at Pimlico Race Course on the day before the Preakness. (Michael J. Marten/Horsephotos)

Michael Matz *(right)*, Peter Brette, and I stand on the grass as the horses are saddled before the Preakness Stakes on May 20, 2006. Barbaro was acting a bit strange, but not enough to cause concern. (Michael J. Marten/Horsephotos)

A pair of outriders helps me control Barbaro after he broke through the starting gate prematurely at the Preakness. (Horsephotos)

Shortly into the Preakness, I could tell that something was wrong with Barbaro. I pulled him up, hopped off him, and tried to bring him to a full stop as quickly as possible. (Uli Seit/Horsephotos)

Moments after Barbaro's breakdown, I tell Roy Jackson, Gretchen Jackson, and Michael Matz what happened: I just felt the horse go weak. (Michael J. Marten/Horsephotos)

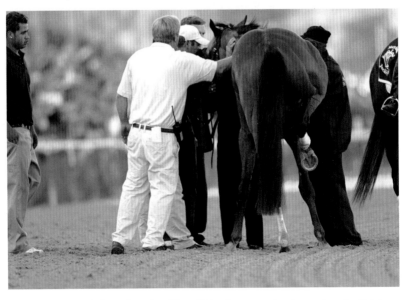

Barbaro instinctively keeps his injured leg off the dirt as veterinarians and track officials tend to him. His intelligence and quick thinking saved his life. (Uli Seit/Horsephotos)

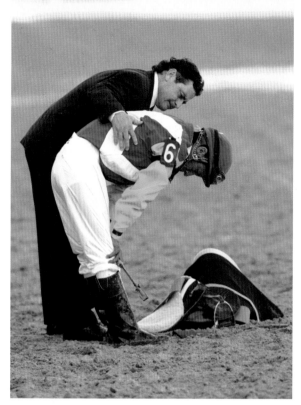

Peter Brette consoles me on the track after the breakdown. All I could do was tell him how sorry I was . . . and cry. (Bill Roberts/ Horsephotos)

Fans at Pimlico distraught over Barbaro's breakdown. I had never seen the public react with such emotion to a horse's injury. (Uli Seit/Horsephotos)

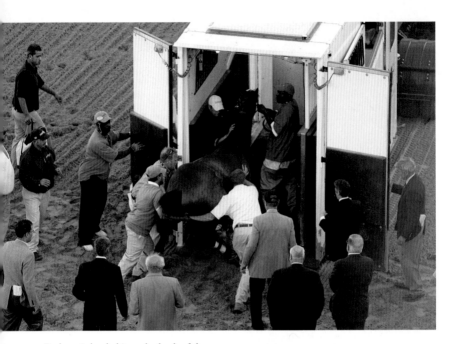

Barbaro is loaded into the back of the
horse ambulance. Later that evening,
the van took him to the New Bolton
Center, the animal hospital in Kennett
Square, Pennsylvania, where he
would spend the next eight months.
(Horsephotos)

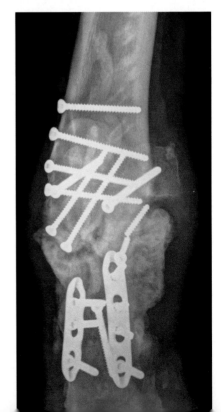

A chilling X ray of Barbaro's fractured
leg after surgery. More bolts than
Frankenstein's skull. (Horsephotos)

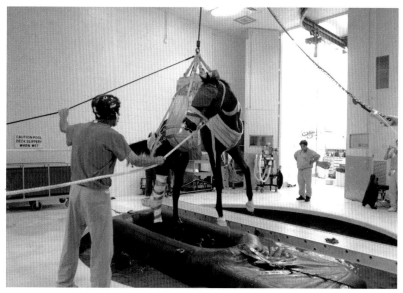

Barbaro is lifted out of the recovery pool after coming out of surgery. The folks at the New Bolton Center did an amazing job treating him during the months he was there. (Sabina Louise Pierce/University of Pennsylvania)

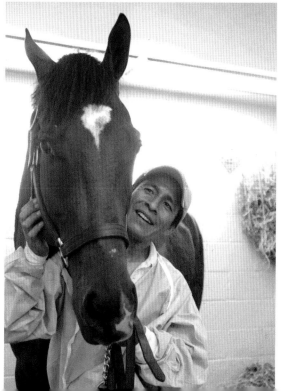

I'm delighted to see Barbaro looking so good on my first visit to the New Bolton Center on May 30, 2006, just ten days after the disastrous Preakness. He seemed happy to see me, too. (Sabina Louise Pierce/University of Pennsylvania)

The New Bolton Center was overwhelmed with get-well-soon messages after Barbaro arrived. (Sabina Louise Pierce/University of Pennsylvania)

I am the first to sign the "World's Largest Get-Well Card" on June 10, 2006, the morning of the Belmont Stakes, three weeks after Barbaro's breakdown. By the end of the day, thousands of people had followed my lead. (Harold Roth/Horsephotos)

Dr. Dean Richardson and I graze Barbaro at the New Bolton Center on September 19, 2006. I thought for sure he was going to make it. (Liliana Prado)

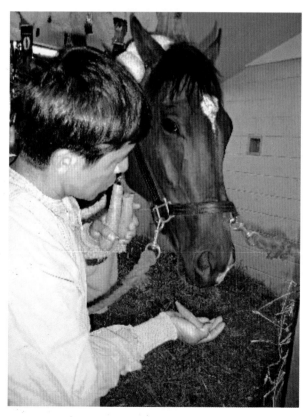

I feed carrots to Barbaro, who always loved to snack. (Liliana Prado)

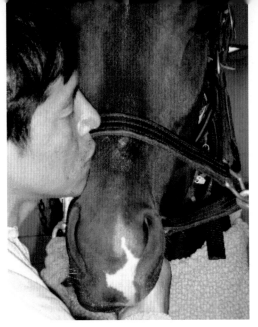

Barbaro lets me kiss and hug him at the New Bolton Center. If I'd known this would be the last time I'd see him, I would have held on for longer. (Liliana Prado)

Despite the ups and downs of his final months, I will always remember Barbaro as the gorgeous champion who touched my life and the lives of so many others. (Horsephotos/ Michael J. Marten)

My heart pounded as I eased him out of the pack and veered toward the outer rail. Was this really happening? Was I dreaming?

What if Barbaro turned out to be fine and I had just pulled up a healthy horse with a chance to win the Triple Crown? I was willing to take the heat. Looking back later, I was just glad I had enough respect in the industry that I felt safe taking the risk. A younger or less experienced jockey, one who hadn't accomplished as much, might not have felt as confident, fearing the criticism he would face if the horse turned out to be healthy. That could have been disastrous. If Barbaro had kept going for just another fifty yards, he might have suffered a worse injury like a compound leg fracture—a broken bone that pierces the skin, often leading to an infection. Horses seldom survive that. They're often given a lethal injection—put down—right on the track.

As I pulled the reins and Barbaro drifted out and slowed, I looked back and down and saw he was running on three legs, favoring his right rear. He was so driven and so athletic that he still wanted to run hard, no doubt hating the sight of the others pulling away. He wanted to go with them and beat them!

But I kept jerking the reins and he finally stopped near the finish line, in the shadow of the packed grandstand. The crowd had let loose a deafening roar when the starting gate opened moments earlier, but now it was silent. I glanced over at the fans in the first rows. They stared at us, barely able to believe what they were seeing. Some of their mouths hung open.

I jumped off Barbaro and put both of my hands on him to try to control him. Some injured horses lash out, but Barbaro let me hold him. He didn't want to get away. It was like he trusted me, knew I was trying to help. Even in the most painful of moments, he was so smart.

As I held him, I looked down and saw him dangling his right hind leg awkwardly over the dirt. That was the first indication this might be bad. I hoped it wasn't broken. I didn't see blood, so it wasn't a compound fracture. I had hope. Maybe it was a minor injury and he would live to race another day.

Later, commentators praised me for acting fast and helping Barbaro survive, but the horse did it by himself. Even though he surely felt panic and pain, he remained calm enough to follow my instructions and let me control him. And somehow, he had the instinct to raise his injured leg over the dirt and keep it from getting infected.

For a few moments, it was just the two of us alone on the track, but then we had company—lots of it. A member of the track operations crew came running up and put his hands on the horse's neck, hoping to help me control him. Then, Jose, Barbaro's groom, reached us. Fortunately, the horse had stopped not far from where he stood, near the winner's circle.

"*Que paso?*" Jose shouted as he took the reins. What happened?

I shrugged. I had no idea.

Veterinarians and track officials soon arrived in waves. The equine ambulance pulled up. The track became an accident scene. Michael and Peter raced from the stands, arriving within seconds, followed quickly by the Jacksons. Everyone hovered around Barbaro.

The rest of the Preakness field circled the track, came through the stretch, and crossed the finish line, Bernardini winning with ease in what had to be the least-watched Preakness in years. Nobody clapped or cheered. All eyes were on Barbaro, as had been the case since I pulled him up.

Some of the track employees formed a shield to keep Barbaro from seeing the other horses as they finished and ran by us—the sight might excite him and cause him to jump, further damaging his leg. But he was too smart for that. He didn't flinch. He was calm.

As I stood nearby on the dirt, Peter came over wearing the saddest of looks—face ashen, eyes downcast. I almost burst into tears when I saw him. He embraced me, and I sputtered the only words that came to mind: "I'm so sorry, Peter, just so sorry."

People kept asking what had happened. I kept saying he just didn't feel right. Finally, I stepped back, put my head in my hands, and bent over. What a nightmare.

When I stood back up, I looked over at the stands and saw a woman crying. Then, as the vets continued to work on Barbaro, a track official took out the green mesh screen they put up to keep people from seeing when they put a horse down on the track.

"Oh, my God," I thought.

A man in the stands shouted exactly what I was thinking: "Don't you put that horse down! Not now!"

Try to save him, in other words. Give him a chance.

Later, I found out they never intended to put him down there; the track official had opened the screen as standard procedure, and quickly folded it back up when Michael explained that it was flapping in the wind and the noise was upsetting Barbaro.

I stayed with Barbaro until he was loaded into the equine ambulance and taken away, headed for his stall in the stakes barn. I stumbled up to the jockeys' room to shower. I knew NBC wanted me to come on camera and speak, but I was in no shape for that. I was in a daze, my mind racing. What had happened? What could I have done? What was going to happen to Barbaro?

Some reporters came in, and I answered one or two questions, but I couldn't continue. I just wanted to go see Barbaro at the stakes barn. The whole time I was showering and changing, I thought, "When I get over there, I hope I see him standing in his stall like nothing had happened." But that was a fantasy.

When I got to the barn, the scene was beyond crazy. Hundreds of onlookers had gathered. Security guards were everywhere. A helicopter buzzed overhead. People were running around. I got through the layers of people and reached the barn. Everyone on the "team" was there—the Jacksons, Michael, Peter, and four or five vets. A team of X-ray technicians was inside the stall, taking pictures of Barbaro's leg.

Everyone hugged me, and I asked how the horse was doing. There was a pause, and then Nick Meittinis, a local vet whom I knew, gave me the bad news.

"Edgar, I'm sorry," he said. "But it doesn't look good at all."

I think the look on my face told him my heart was breaking.

The X-ray pictures were devastating, he said. Barbaro's right rear leg bones had shattered into more little pieces than anyone could count—at least two dozen. Putting all that back together would be close to impossible.

"But you're going to try everything, right? Please?" I asked, my heart pounding loud in my ears.

I was praying they wouldn't put him down.

The doctor replied, "You can only do so much, Edgar. It's a very, very bad break."

But then the doctor told me the Jacksons had decided that, in spite of the odds, they wanted to try to save the horse—or at least explore the possibility. They knew it wouldn't be easy for Barbaro to beat such a bad injury and resume a normal life, much less race again, but they felt he deserved the chance. His skin had, in fact, remained sealed, so there was a smaller risk of infection. At least there was some good news.

It looked like the horse would be going to the New Bolton Center, a University of Pennsylvania veterinary hospital in Kennett Square, Pennsylvania, outside Philadelphia—about ninety miles away. There was talk of him undergoing surgery as soon as possible.

I walked over to Barbaro's stall and stepped inside. I don't know if the look on my face scared them, but the vets, Jose, and the X-ray techs all left. Barbaro and I were alone, suddenly. He gave me a warm look and I started crying, actually bawling, big tears rolling down my cheeks. This was supposed to have been a great day, one of the best ever, but look what it had come to.

Barbaro rested his head on my shoulder. I don't know what he was thinking—I'm pretty sure he was in pain—but I just held him, and he relaxed his head on my shoulder; I think he was glad I was there. We stayed in that position for at least five minutes, together in our private world amid all the noise and chaos outside. Then one of the vets walked in and said they were ready to take the horse to the New Bolton Center.

I nodded, stepped back, and said good-bye to my friend. Jose took him, and as I wiped away my tears, he led Barbaro out of the stall and into the back of the ambulance. The Kentucky Derby winner was hopping on his three good legs.

CHAPTER 11

"Be Brave, Barbaro"

When I left Pimlico, I got in my car and headed toward Javier's place in Woodstock. Once I was outside the city, the highway gave way to dark rural roads. I drove and drove. I wasn't hungry or thirsty, didn't want to stop, didn't want to talk. I needed time to take everything in. Barbaro was on his way to the New Bolton Center. No one knew if he would survive the night.

People who work in horse racing accept breakdowns as an unfortunate part of the business. I was familiar with the experience. But to have a Kentucky Derby winner go down under me before 118,000 people and a national TV audience, and to have so many grand hopes and dreams dashed completely within a span of seconds—this was all new, and too much to take. I just felt shattered.

I drove aimlessly, going up and down dark roads. My cell phone rang and rang, but I didn't pick up. I was in some sort of state. I thought about my mother. What would she have said at this moment? I thought back to when Barbaro and I had won the Kentucky Derby just two weeks earlier. How could things have gone so wrong so quickly?

Finally I came out of it. Liliana called from Javier's house. I picked up. "Where are you?" Liliana cried. "The phone is ringing, everyone is crying. Are you OK?"

I told her I was fine, just driving around and thinking. She asked if I would be home soon. I promised I would.

When I got to the house, my relatives gathered around the kitchen table and compared horror stories. Liliana, Patty, and Louis had spent the afternoon in a corporate tent in the infield. They watched the start of the Preakness on TV, but when I pulled Barbaro up, NBC stayed with the race and they couldn't see me. Patty thought maybe something had happened to her father. She bolted for the track and got as far as the inner rail, but a security guard wouldn't let her go farther. Louis stayed with Liliana and barely said a word, his eyes filled with tears, his lips trembling.

I knew everyone wanted to hear my version of what happened, but I didn't have it in me to speak. I just went to bed.

I slept fitfully, tossing and turning as I replayed Saturday's various scenes—the premature breakthrough, the moment when I pulled Barbaro up, the moment when I learned how seriously he was injured. There was nothing I could do about any of it now.

Early the next morning, my family and I got up and went to the airport. Liliana, Patty, and Louis flew back to Florida. I had mounts that afternoon at Belmont. As I waited for my flight to New York, I watched a news show on a TV in the departure lounge. Barbaro's breakdown was one of the top stories. There was video of me pulling up the horse, just what I didn't want to see.

I would be flying from New York to Florida later that evening to spend a couple of days off with Liliana and the kids, and honestly, I wanted to take this day off, too. But it would be unprofessional to take off once I had committed to ride. I would get myself ready. This was how I made my living, and I couldn't begin making exceptions—not now, not ever.

When I arrived at Belmont, I glanced at the newspapers in the jockeys' room. Barbaro was all over the headlines. There were pictures of me and pictures of the horse, all taken on the track. I couldn't get away from it.

Before the first race, I called Michael, who was at the New Bolton Center with the Jacksons. Michael updated me on what had happened since last night. Barbaro was now in a stall in the center's intensive care unit. His ride up from Pimlico the night before had gone well. Jose stood beside him the whole way in the back of the ambulance. People on the route saw on TV that he was coming and draped bedsheets on overpasses saying "Good Luck" and "We Love You, Barbaro." A TV news helicopter followed the van up the highway, broadcasting live shots. Cable channels broke into their programming to follow the story. The horse arrived safely at the clinic, hopped into the ICU, and had slept and eaten well since being admitted.

He seemed comfortable, Michael said, and the Jacksons had officially decided to go ahead and try to repair his leg. A well-known surgeon, Dr. Dean Richardson, would operate.

The three main bones in the right rear leg had shattered into twenty-seven pieces—twenty-seven!—and putting them back together would be unbelievably hard. But Michael was upbeat.

"Everything is good so far, Edgar," he said. "He's stable. I think he'll be in surgery today."

I felt better, but then I went out for the first race, and people booed me because of what had happened to Barbaro. I couldn't believe it.

Racing fans usually just move on to the next race, regardless of what happens. But on this Sunday in New York, fans stood at the railing and shouted angry things at me.

"It's your fault that horse got hurt!" one yelled.

Sitting on my mount before the first race, I looked at him with wide eyes. I was floored. I didn't respond. I didn't know how.

Hearing this man blame me made me want to change my plans, cancel my mounts for a week, just get away, take the family to Peru, and have some quiet time. But then I thought, You didn't take time off when your mother died; you should stick it out now. I knew if I went to Peru, I wouldn't be able to relax. I would be restless, nervous. It wasn't worth it.

I made it through the race and the rest of the day without being booed again. At one point I heard on a TV in the jockeys' room that Barbaro was in surgery. I called Michael after my last mount. He walked me through what had happened.

Barbaro had been put into a full-body sling, knocked out with anesthesia, and carried to the operating table on a gurney that ran on a monorail attached to the ceiling. Dr. Richardson had opened up his leg. The details of the injury were amazing. Barbaro had broken pretty much everything in his lower leg—the long and short pasterns, the cannon bone, and sesa-moids—and had also dislocated the fetlock joint, which con-nected the cannon to the pasterns. The long pastern alone had broken into twenty pieces. It had taken the doctor five hours to put everything back together using a steel plate and twenty-seven screws.

When Dr. Richardson was finished, Barbaro was trans-ported by the monorail from the operating room to a re-covery pool filled with warm water. Horses waking up from anesthesia tend to thrash and kick because they're scared, so at New Bolton doctors put them in a deep pool, where they can kick without hurting themselves. Then they pull them from the pool and force them to stand to see if the repaired limb can bear weight.

Barbaro had awakened in the water, and once he was out, stood right up and practically jogged back to his stall with a weight-bearing fiberglass cast on the injured leg. Incredibly, he could stand on all four feet again. Having watched him hop into the ambulance on three legs less than twenty-four hours earlier, I could hardly believe it.

This was all great news. But Dr. Richardson was being realistic, Michael said, and trying not to get people's hopes too high. He had told the press that Barbaro's survival was still a "coin toss" because of the possibility of infection or other complications such as laminitis, a painful hoof disease that sometimes sets in when a horse can't distribute its weight evenly on all four legs. We wouldn't know for months whether Barbaro would survive, Dr. Richardson said.

I felt better after hearing all that, even though I knew

Barbaro was facing a long, tough road. He deserved the chance to live. He would never race again and probably couldn't father sons and daughters, either—he would have to put all of his weight, more than 1,200 pounds, on his back legs to enter a mare, and it was doubtful his damaged leg could carry such a load—but the world was full of horses that lived happily in pastures for years. I knew the Jacksons would be thrilled if Barbaro could have that kind of life; it was the least they could do for a horse that had given them so many thrills. It was the least any of us could do.

After I spoke to Michael, I checked my cell phone to see who had called, and my voice mail was full. I sat at my locker, tired and sweaty, and listened to condolence messages that had come in from all over the world.

Roberto Alvarez Calderon, the president of the Monterrico racetrack in Peru, said, "Being close to you, we want you to know we are feeling the same pain you're feeling now. Horse racing in Peru is in tears over what has happened to this potential Triple Crown winner."

Andreas Suborics, a German jockey I had met and befriended at the World Racing Championships in Japan, sent me a text message: "I saw what was surely a painful event for you, and I want you to know I'm feeling your pain with you." Kieron Fallon, an Irish jockey, left a voice message with a similar thought. Many friends, in and out of racing, left messages, some while crying so hard I couldn't even understand them. I was deeply moved by the responses, and for the first time, began to grasp that Barbaro's breakdown had had a powerful impact on people.

That evening I flew to Florida to spend two days off with Liliana and the kids. I thought I would get at least a little break, but when I got to Florida, the phone was ringing every five minutes. Reporters from everywhere were calling—TV, print, radio. I told Liliana I didn't want to talk to any of them. The congratulatory interviews following the Derby had elated me, but now I dreaded speaking to the same people.

Liliana knocked some sense into me. "You better talk to these people, Edgar," she said. "They have questions, and they're going to wonder if something happened during the race and maybe blame you."

So I called everyone back, talked to CNN, ABC, radio stations, the papers. I went through the breakdown again and again. That was brutal. I pride myself on my ability to read my horses, and I hated that I hadn't spotted a signal, a little sign that told me, "OK, don't run." I knew something wasn't quite right during the post parade, but unfortunately, it wasn't enough to alarm me. And now Barbaro was fighting for his life. I felt terribly about not having been able to help him.

On Wednesday, after a couple nights of tossing and turning, I flew back to New York to ride for the rest of the week. To my surprise, I began receiving sympathy cards and letters, at first a trickle, and then a flood. They came to me at the track, at home (in Florida as well as New York), and as I learned later, at the California offices of the Jockeys Guild, our union. Hundreds of people wanted me to know how sorry they were about Barbaro, and how grateful they were that I had helped him.

Dear Mr. Prado:

Thank you so much for guiding Barbaro to his victories, and for taking care of him in the Preakness. You saved his life. I heard some people mistreated you at Belmont Park. They are idiots. You are the No. 1 jockey in America, and more importantly, a fine example. I know your heart is broken over Barbaro, as are ours, but please know people are praying for you.

—*Amarillo, Texas*

Sir:

Barbaro was a strong racing champion but he was like a little child needing help when he broke down at Pimlico. You should be so proud of what you did. The sorrow expressed on your face was an unmistakable indication of the devastation you're feeling inside. I started crying when I watched a replay of the NBC broadcast. Your face spoke for millions of people, but no one else could have done what you did. Thank you.

—*Sarasota, Florida*

Edgar:

It took infinite wisdom and skill to handle Barbaro as deftly as you did at Pimlico. You have won thousands of races, but now you have given a majestic champion (hopefully) the gift of life. Your mother would be so proud.

—*Atlanta, Georgia*

With their words as comfort, I slowly settled back into the daily racing grind at Belmont. But I was thinking about Barbaro all the time—and I was far from alone. As my mail intimated, there was an incredible swell of public interest in the horse's condition. I had never seen anything like it. Barbaro's rise and fall had touched a public nerve I had never even known existed.

In just the few days since the Preakness, hundreds of people had posted messages on the Web site of Tim Woolley, a Delaware Park trainer based at Fair Hill. One of his exercise riders, Alex Brown, had been posting Barbaro updates before the Preakness because he was a fan of the horse, and the site had been receiving about 150 hits a day. Brown had planned to take the site down after Barbaro broke down, but he logged on the next day and discovered it was receiving 3,000 hits an hour while Barbaro was in surgery. People across the county had come to the site, wanting to know the latest on the horse. Brown kept the site up, and it had quickly become a place for people to express their sadness, love, and support.

"We are devastated!" wrote a fan from Columbus, Ohio. "Each season's crop of Triple Crown competitors brings hopes for a new equine superhero such as splendid Barbaro, nurtured and supported by outstanding humans such as the Jacksons, Michael Matz, Peter Brette, and quick-witted Edgar Prado. Accidents such as this are heart-breaking reminders that even superheroes are vulnerable. We pray that Barbaro will recover, sire equally wonderful colts and fillies, and live a long, pampered life."

The New Bolton Center's Web site had also become a

popular gathering place for fans wanting to show support and send online get-well messages to Barbaro. "We don't have a keyboard in his stall yet, so I don't know how that is going to work out," Dr. Richardson said with a smile. But the clinic was putting out daily updates on the horse's condition, and its site was receiving thousands of hits a day, as opposed to five hundred to a thousand per day before the Preakness.

And the mail I was receiving represented just a fraction of what was being sent to Barbaro himself. Hundreds of cards, letters, posters, banners, and flower baskets had been delivered to the New Bolton Center, along with enough candy, apples, and baby carrots (Barbaro's favorite treat) to fill several tubs. People were sending stuffed animals, prayer candles, holy water, treatment suggestions, and most importantly, in one case, an anonymous half-million-dollar gift. The center had used the latter to start the Barbaro Fund, with proceeds going to the care of all of its animals.

What had caused this explosion of sentiment? Why this horse? It was hard to say for sure. Great horses had broken down before on national television. The brilliant filly Go For Wand was put down on the track after shattering her ankle approaching the finish line in the 1990 Breeders' Cup Distaff. The 1993 Preakness winner, Prairie Bayou, went down three weeks later in the Belmont. The most famous modern breakdown—until now, at least—was that of Ruffian, an unbeaten filly who shattered both of the sesamoid bones in her right foreleg in a Belmont Park match race against Foolish Pleasure, the 1975 Kentucky Derby winner. She kept running because she had never been behind and hated the feeling, but finally couldn't continue. Surgeons repaired the leg that evening, but she woke up thrashing wildly, as if she was still racing, and broke her cast and another leg. She finally was put down, and her death haunted fans for years. Yet I don't think even that could match the emotional response to Barbaro's injury, which was coming not just from racing fans and horse lovers, but also from non–sports fans, people who otherwise wouldn't care.

I had my own theory about why this was happening. Barbaro had shown he was a special talent, maybe a horse for the ages; it certainly had been years since one won the Kentucky Derby so impressively. And he was more than just fast—he was smart, charismatic, the breed at its finest. But just as he was set to deliver on his promise, he had been cut down, robbed of the opportunity to perform. Little in this world is more depressing than potential going unfulfilled, but unlike Ruffian or Go For Wand, he had survived, so you could root for him to make it.

His sudden and tragic reversal of fortune was a reminder of how fragile life is—you could be on top one second and fighting for your life the next. Tens of thousands of people experience similarly dramatic swings every day, just not on TV or in the spotlight. They're told they have cancer, or their spouse walks out, or their stock portfolio drops. One way or another, the bottom falls out of their lives, just as the bottom had fallen out of Barbaro's, and now, like them, Barbaro was setting out to make the most of it—or at least, survive. Anyone who has hit bottom and tried to dig himself out from bad times could relate.

Plus, he was just an animal, genuine and earnest but unable to communicate his feelings. We had so many questions for him, suddenly. Was he in pain? Did he think he would survive? Was he aware of the support he was receiving? There is an old saying that you always want what you can't have, and we would never hear Barbaro's answers. To fill that void, we could only imagine what he would say, and convince ourselves we were helping by expressing support.

A week after the Preakness I called Dr. Richardson to express my thanks and also to find out from him what the horse's long-term prospects were. We had a nice but brief conversation. He was a busy man. I decided it would be easier to get the latest news from Michael or the Jacksons. The Jacksons lived four miles from the New Bolton Center, and Gretchen was there all the time. She filled me in whenever I called, which was often. "How are we doing?" I would ask. She would say everything was going OK, and Barbaro was standing and eating well.

I needed to go see him myself. Thinking about him made me emotional. I owe so much to the horses I ride. They have brought me everything I have, given me their all, risked their lives for me. My whole existence—my children's futures—depends on them. And now, the one that had given me my biggest thrill, the greatest victory, was fighting for his life.

He wasn't far away, but I was riding every day, so it was hard to find time to make the trip to go see him. I studied my schedule. Memorial Day was coming up, and that meant a long weekend of racing, but afterward I had a couple of days off. I picked out the Tuesday after Memorial Day to go, just by myself. But I told a few people of my plans, and I soon heard from the National Thoroughbred Racing Association, the organization that promotes American racing. The TV show *Good Morning America* wanted to tape me seeing Barbaro for the first time since the Preakness. Obviously, I couldn't have that private visit I wanted—the story was just too big. I said I would do it. Barbaro was doing well, and if my visit brought positive attention to racing and to this great horse, I was all for it.

The NTRA made it easy. Peter Rotondo from their communications department traveled with me. He arranged for a stretch limousine to take us. We met at Belmont at 5:30 a.m. on that Tuesday. I got in and immediately fell asleep. I had ridden in eight races the day before, including the Met Mile, which I won. Between my riding schedule and the Barbaro hoopla, I was exhausted.

The distance from Belmont to the clinic was about 150 miles. The roads were empty, and I slept most of the way, but when I awoke, I felt happy to be going to visit Barbaro. We had developed a bond, and all I had done since we were together in his stall at Pimlico was talk to Michael and Gretchen about him. I needed to see him myself. I hoped he looked as good as they said he did.

The New Bolton Center was a low-key campus of one-story buildings in the countryside west of Philadelphia, just north of the Delaware line. Aside from the hospital, the facility included a vet school and a research center. Horse-farm fencing surrounded it, so for the most part the center looked no different from the neighboring farms. But you knew you were there when you pulled into the driveway. You couldn't miss it. The front fence, running alongside the road, had been turned into a Barbaro shrine.

Dozens of homemade posters and banners were tacked up. One large, square white board read "Be Brave, Barbaro," with the words written in the Jacksons' blue-and-green colors. Another read "Believe In Barbaro," also in green and blue. There was a large brown rectangular poster, two feet by three feet, featuring pictures of the horse and the words "God Bless Barbaro, Get Well Soon." Another read "We Believe in Barbaro" and was signed by "the Barbaromaniacs." Flower baskets and stuffed animals were propped up at the foot of the fence.

When Peter and I got out of the limo and went inside, we saw there was another shrine, just as large, in the entry hallway. The woman working the front desk said the clinic was being bombarded, receiving dozens of packages a day with more presents than could be displayed.

I laughed to myself, thinking of my desire for a quiet visit; this place was a madhouse. Peter and I were taken to a conference room. Dr. Richardson walked in and introduced himself. We compared notes on the horse. He was amazed at Barbaro's intelligence, how calm the horse was, and how well he adapted to whatever situation he was put in. The doctor had been around horses forever, and he knew this was a special one.

Dr. Richardson showed me before-and-after X-rays of the broken leg. Before surgery, the bones looked like the crushed ice you get from a vending machine in a hotel; it was sickening to realize they were real. But in the X-rays taken after the surgery, the bones were back together, connected by so many bolts sticking out in all directions that it looked like an X-ray of Frankenstein's skull. The doctor told me the surgery had gone perfectly, and Barbaro seemed to be happy and pain-free. I thanked him.

The time had come to visit Barbaro. Excited but a bit nervous, I walked out of the front building, down a sidewalk, and stopped just inside the door to the ICU. I put on hospital scrubs to minimize the possibility of infection, as everyone did when they went into the ICU.

With the TV cameras rolling, I walked through a set of double doors, into the ICU, and over to Barbaro's stall, which was in the corner.

"Hey, guy!" I chirped. "How you doing, guy?"

He reacted immediately, came to me like an old friend. I don't pretend to know how horses think, but I swear he knew me. His ears pricked, and he let me hold him and pat him. My eyes filled with tears.

I wondered if he remembered me from his races and thought my presence meant he was getting ready to run again. He looked ready. His coat was shiny. He was alert, bright-eyed, and looking around, as if to say, "Hey, I'm going to make it, don't worry." There was none of the droopy-eyed look you got with horses on a lot of pain medication. Frankly, he seemed the same in every way other than the cast on his leg and the intravenous drip pouch attached to his side by a needle.

His stall was roomy enough, about twelve by fifteen feet, with walls painted a peach color and a pair of square windows at the back. Right by the front door, the staff had filled a basket with some of the sweets, carrots, and fruit he had received. It was fine to give him anything out of the basket, they said, because he would be struggling to keep his weight up after surgery.

I met the nurses who were taking care of him, all women except for a Spanish-speaking guy named Ray Gonzales. He came up with a shy smile and introduced himself in Spanish, and we hit it off. I asked him a lot of questions. What did he think of Barbaro? Was he an easy horse to take care of? Was he eating well? Drinking a lot of water? Was he happy?

Ray said he was a dream to care for, adaptable and willing. Ray was blown away by his combination of size and intelligence. What an animal, he said. He told me the horse was learning to live with that cast, and with having to be inside all the time. Whenever he heard a noise, he went over and looked through the window. He was as curious as ever. I told Ray to take care of him, and to call if he ever wanted to talk.

I stayed in the ICU for an hour. Barbaro was upbeat the whole time. I talked to him, petted him, fed him baby carrots. He put his head on my shoulder again, just as he had at Pimlico. We had ourselves a grand time as the TV cameras rolled.

The NTRA had called a press conference with me, Dr. Richardson, and the Jacksons. After leaving the ICU, I went to a room packed with reporters from around the country. Dr. Richardson did most of the talking. "Barbaro has had an incredibly good week," he said. "He's done far better than we ever could have hoped for—so far, so far, so far."

He went back over the details of the reconstruction and

explained that the cast would be changed every few weeks. He was mostly worried about the injured leg becoming infected, and about laminitis developing in the other hind leg.

"There's no question things are better but he is still a long, long way from being discharged," Dr. Richardson said. "All these bad things could still happen. But bone is the only tissue in the body that can heal and be truly stronger. He won't have normal mobility but the bone will be very strong."

When a reporter asked for my impressions, I said I was encouraged. And I was. Part of me had been afraid to see Barbaro, thinking he might appear weak or depressed. But he looked like he could run in the Belmont Stakes in a couple of weeks except for that darn cast.

"I was heartbroken after the Preakness, and it is going to take a long time for that to heal," I said. "But he is doing better."

Michael wasn't at New Bolton that morning; he was at Fair Hill, working his horses. Roy Jackson suggested we meet there, which sounded great to me. Aside from the fact that it would be nice for "the team" to be together again after all we had been through, Michael had received a DVD from Pimlico that had various views of Barbaro's breakdown, including the stewards' films. Lou Raffetto, the president of Pimlico, had told the press after studying the films that he thought Barbaro had clipped heels with a horse running behind him, Brother Derek, and that had caused Barbaro to take an awkward step. I wanted to see the films.

In the ten days since the race, I had heard countless theories about what caused Barbaro to break down. Some people thought he had taken a bad step because the track itself wasn't groomed well. I didn't buy that. I rode on that track all day, and it was fine; Pimlico does a great job caring for its track. Other people were convinced Barbaro had injured himself when he broke through the gate too soon. I didn't believe that, either. In the first place, he broke through with his front legs and injured a back leg. Also, Dr. Zipf and I both examined him before he went back in, and he was fine. And while he certainly didn't run well in the first hundred yards, he wasn't running on a fractured leg.

No, something happened a hundred yards into the race, when I suddenly felt him weaken. Had he clipped heels with Brother Derek? I had my doubts. But if not, what had caused the injury?

Peter Rotondo and I took our limo to Fair Hill and met up with Michael. The Jacksons were already there. Michael gave me a tour of his barn and showed me the training track. I understood why Barbaro had been so happy there. It was a horse's paradise, worlds away from the bustle of the racetrack.

Then we all watched the DVD in Michael's office. We went back and forth looking at views of the breakdown—from the side, head-on, high, low. We agreed that, with all due respect to the people at Pimlico, we didn't see clear evidence that Barbaro and Brother Derek had clipped heels. Something other than that probably was to blame. But what? I realized even then that we probably would never know.

After a while Peter and I said our good-byes, got in the limo, and headed back to New York. It was mid-afternoon, and we had been so busy that we had forgotten to eat. We pulled over at a fast-food place, got some lunch, and ate in the back as the driver headed north. We laughed at ourselves, eating fast-food burgers in the back of a stretch limo.

I felt better than I had at any moment since the Preakness. What a joy it had been to see Barbaro in such good spirits and good shape. Since his breakdown, my mind had kept going back to that image of him hopping into the ambulance on three legs—one of the saddest sights I had ever seen. Now, at least I had newer, happier images to reflect on. I would never stop feeling terrible, but for the first time, I felt he would survive.

CHAPTER 12

He Stole My Heart

When you're getting into this business, you learn from experienced "racetrackers" not to get too attached to any particular horse. That's the first commandment. Be careful, you're told, they'll only break your heart. This is a tough, competitive business, not a romance novel. If you're a jockey, just get on them, get off them, and move on.

That doesn't mean you can't love them all, as I do, having been taught to appreciate these beautiful animals by my father years ago. But you can't get too attached to any one. I had that drummed into me until it became as much a part of me as my flesh and blood. Forget whatever just happened, I was told, because there's always another race coming up. Focus on your next horse.

As I have gone through my racing life, a few horses have naturally stood out—Leariva, Lemon Drop Kid, Birdstone. They helped me climb important rungs on the ladder, and I loved them for what they did. But I didn't become too attached.

Then Barbaro came along, and I found myself breaking that first commandment—and not just breaking it, but shattering it into a thousand little pieces, like a stone tablet that had been hurled to the ground.

I couldn't just get on Barbaro, get off him, and move on. I loved him too much.

It wasn't just that he had done so much for me. It was the way he came to me when he saw me, ears pricked, anxious to communicate. It was the warm look in his eyes when he heard my voice. It was his sense of humor, the way he teased me when I fed him a baby carrot, looking away and then swooping back in with a gulp.

It was what I saw in my mind when I closed my eyes and thought about him charging through the stretch at Churchill Downs, the whole world watching him take great gulps of ground, his competition falling away.

We were kindred spirits, as alike in some ways as fraternal twins. I didn't have his talent, but he had given everything he had to racing, including his life, almost, and I had given my all, too, seldom turning down any opportunity, large or small. We both loved the game, the competition. When I got on him before a race, I knew he was excited, and he knew I was just as excited.

As soon as I got home from the New Bolton Center after that first visit, my goal was to get back to see him as soon as possible. I hadn't broken the commandment forbidding me from becoming too attached to one horse. Barbaro had broken it for me. He gave me no choice. He stole my heart.

When Liliana, Patty, and Louis joined me for the summer

in New York after school let out in Florida, they wanted to go see him, too. They had been as shaken as anyone by the breakdown, and of course, it was more personal for them because Barbaro had brought our family such joy. Patty had written the Jacksons a wonderful note expressing her sadness.

We couldn't get there before the Belmont Stakes, the final leg of the Triple Crown, which was held at Belmont three weeks after the Preakness and eleven days after I visited New Bolton. Having lost my Triple Crown horse, I picked up the mount on Deputy Glitters, a colt that had won the Tampa Bay Derby earlier that spring and finished eighth in the Kentucky Derby. He went off at 12–1 in the Belmont and finished nowhere. With Bernardini skipping the race, it was won by Jazil, the colt that had run fourth in the Kentucky Derby. As his connections gathered in the winner's circle, I couldn't help thinking how this should have been the moment when Barbaro completed his Triple Crown sweep. He had destroyed Jazil in Kentucky, finishing ten lengths ahead. Jazil never would have beaten him in the Belmont.

Oh, what could have been.

The best thing that happened on Belmont Saturday came before the first race. The NTRA had come up with the idea of sending Barbaro what it called "the world's largest get-well card"—a banner seven feet high and sixty-two feet long, featuring four large pictures of Barbaro. It was hung on a wall in the stands, and fans could sign it and send Barbaro their best wishes. The NTRA asked me to be the first person to sign it. I put on the Jacksons' silks, went down at 10:00 a.m., and signed my name and "Love, Forever." By the end of the day, thousands of people had signed their names and expressed their support. I knew I would see the banner on the front fence at the New Bolton Center soon enough.

It had been three weeks since the Preakness, and the interest in Barbaro was, if anything, becoming more intense. If tears could cure a horse, he would already be out of the clinic and back in training. Thousands of messages had been posted on the Tim Woolley and New Bolton Center Web sites. The news media was still all over the story, a sure sign of the public's continuing interest. The New Bolton Center was putting out daily updates, mostly saying Barbaro was eating and sleeping well, in no obvious pain, and Dr. Richardson was pleased. The public ate up every morsel of news. Barbaro updates had become part of the daily news cycle, broadcast on all channels and Web sites, printed in every major paper.

Commentators tried to explain what was now being called "the Barbaro phenomenon." One column written for *Slate*, an online magazine, suggested the public was obsessed with the horse because America was at war in Iraq, and that the country historically came together behind a horse—a strong, silent hero—during difficult times. The writer pointed out that Secretariat and Ruffian had become famous when Watergate and Vietnam were tearing up the country in the 1970s, and that Seabiscuit rose to fame during the Depression. A few weeks later, a columnist in Denver, Colorado, would write that Barbaro was "everything we wished our human athletes were: silent, brave and brief," reminding us of a simpler time when athletes weren't on steroids and didn't get into so much trouble off the playing fields.

I'm a jockey, not a sociologist. I was mostly just broken-hearted about what had happened to my friend, and also anxious to do whatever I could to make Barbaro feel better. My family felt the same way. On the Monday after the Belmont, we all awoke early, piled into the car, and headed for the New Bolton Center. Patty and Louis slept in the back, and I slept in the passenger seat while Liliana drove. I had the day off from racing, so we didn't have to rush.

Dr. Richardson had changed Barbaro's cast for the first time a few days earlier, and reported that the leg looked great. The doctor had seemed excited about how things were going. He told the press Barbaro was "a bright and lively and happy horse." The clinic was still being flooded with cards, banners, and flowers, but unlike my first visit, there weren't as many reporters around. The place was quiet. This was how I wanted to see Barbaro, with no one else around. I wanted us to be able to communicate privately, as we had on the track.

What we saw that day confirmed what Dr. Richardson had said. Barbaro was in great spirits. When I reached the door of his stall and called his name, he came right to me. I picked a baby carrot out of his treat basket and offered it to him. He snapped it right up. Then I gave him a peppermint, and later, an apple. He was having fun. He took a playful nip at me, which really told me he was feeling like his old self. He had loved to nip at people when he was in training.

I didn't see Dr. Richardson, but I spoke to a handful of the nurses, technicians, and doctors who were taking care of him, including Ray Gonzales, the Spanish-speaking nurse. They took me around the clinic. I saw the operating room where

Dr. Richardson had put Barbaro's leg back together—it was a brightly lit space that looked like a human operating room. I saw the recovery pool where Barbaro came to after surgery. New Bolton was an impressive place.

This time I could sit and visit with the staff. I asked about Barbaro's typical day. He was in the stall all the time, they said, but he had visitors. Gretchen Jackson was coming twice a day with baskets of fresh grass from her farm for him to eat. Gretchen loved the horse so much. Michael also was visiting in the afternoons, after morning training at Fair Hill. He brought in the grain and supplements Barbaro had been eating while in training. The horse was eating four times a day now, at midnight, 6:00 a.m., noon, and 6:00 p.m. Jose, the groom, had also visited several times.

The staffers had been around Barbaro for a month now and were, in a word, amazed. He had immediately adjusted to having a broken leg, to getting up, down, and around with a cast. No one showed him how to do it. He just figured it out. Many horses didn't, they said. But the same qualities that had made Barbaro a great racehorse now made him a remarkable patient. He was resourceful and smart, and had a mind of his own. He had always been a handful in the paddock until his saddle went on, and now, in the same way, he was playful until Dr. Richardson came to the ICU to check on him. He knew Dr. Richardson was the boss, just as he had known Michael was the boss when he was in training. He never messed with the boss.

It was going to cost a small fortune to nurse him back to health in the coming months—imagine a human hospital stay that long, and you start to get the picture—but thankfully, Barbaro wasn't in the hands of a cold syndicate of businessmen who might consider the bottom line. He was in the hands of a pair of incredibly generous and kindhearted horse lovers, the Jacksons.

I'm a horse lover myself. I can't help wishing horse racing was more like it was when it was the "sport of kings," a place for people who loved watching horses run, win or lose; people who smiled when they finished last; people who just loved animals, like the Jacksons, and wanted to be around a horse like Barbaro because he represented the breed at its best. Nothing upsets me more than hearing a jockey say, "I'm here for the money," or "I can't wait to get out of here." Then there are the owners in the game strictly to make money—to put some in and get more in return. They're investors, with no passion for animals. I can't relate to that, and frankly, I find it depressing.

For as much as I learned from my mother, my father instilled in me the love of animals, especially horses, that I feel more than ever today. I think horses are different from God's other creatures. Look at how many ways they have been used through history—as transportation, in battle, the list goes on. Why were they put on Earth? If you throw two hundred in a field, they naturally start running and trying to beat each other. They were put on Earth to race. There have been organized versions of the sport since ancient Rome. It is one of the greatest forms of competition we have.

It is up to us to protect these great athletes so we can keep enjoying them, but unfortunately, we don't always do our part. Some horses are pushed beyond their limits, made to run strictly for financial gain, or given medication so they don't feel pain and can run when they shouldn't. It's wrong. They need rest when they're hurt and should never be medicated just to run in a race. I understand that books need to be balanced, but horses are paying the price. I would love to see people at the top of our sport take a stand, put further limits on medication, and force injured horses to take more time off.

My job is to ride them, take care of them as best I can, and give them a chance to win. Sometimes no amount of protection is enough. Barbaro was totally healthy going into the Preakness, and, thanks to Michael, as rested as any Kentucky Derby champion in years. He was a low injury risk. His breakdown will almost surely be remembered as a freak accident, one of those great mysteries of the turf.

The result was a splendid, special animal reduced to walking around the New Bolton Center with a cast on one leg, his athletic career over but his brilliance and spirit as strong as ever. He put on a show for Liliana, Patty, and Louis when we visited that morning in June. Patty is allergic to horses and Liliana is afraid, but Barbaro flirted with them, let them hold him and feed him snacks. They watched me step inside his stall, pet him, and play with his ears. They felt inspired and moved after seeing him. Barbaro picked you up with his upbeat attitude, his outlook on life. There was every reason to believe he was on the road to recovery.

We ended up staying so long that we ran into Michael, who was making his usual afternoon visit. He invited us to come to his farm for a barbecue. It was a nice offer, and we gladly accepted. Once we got there, Patty and Louis took off for a tree house, and Michael grilled hamburgers and hot dogs. We talked about horses and racing, and of course, Barbaro. The breakdown had devastated Michael more than anyone. No one knew Barbaro better. Michael had spent every day with him, nurtured him, and was still devoted to him, spending as much time as possible visiting him in the clinic. Michael was a true horse lover.

That evening, as Liliana and I drove back to New York with Patty and Louis asleep in the back, Liliana said she wanted to come back and see Barbaro again.

I could hardly wait.

CHAPTER 13

"We're Going to Need a Miracle"

For six weeks after the Preakness, we all lived a fantasy. Barbaro was happy and healing. He spent his days devouring baby carrots and peppermints. He was going to make it.

But it was all a tease. Dr. Richardson had warned that the horse wouldn't be out of danger for months, no matter how well he seemed to be doing. Everyone, including me, forgot about that when the news was all good.

Then, seemingly out of nowhere, in early July, the doctor's fears became real.

Barbaro developed a mild fever and, for the first time, seemed uncomfortable on his hind legs, so he was put under anesthesia for a cast change on July 3. While he was under, Dr. Richardson also went into his leg and replaced two bent screws, and added three more. Barbaro woke up in the recovery pool and returned to his stall. But he still wasn't comfortable, so the doctor changed the cast again two days later and also treated a small abscess on the sole of the horse's uninjured left hoof.

Three days later, the horse developed what Dr. Richardson called "a potentially serious" complication—an infection. The doctor went back in, replaced almost all of the hardware in the broken leg, and changed casts again, this time putting on a longer cast that hopefully would provide more support. But he apparently didn't like what he saw because, two days later, he changed the cast for the third time in a week, this time back to a shorter one. Barbaro had had five casts so far.

But all that was just a warm-up for the bombshell Dr. Richardson dropped on July 13—Barbaro had developed severe laminitis in his left hind hoof. My stomach dropped when Michael called with the news. In my experience, horses with laminitis seldom lived for more than a week. It was often a death sentence.

Laminitis was an extremely painful and somewhat mysterious ailment that usually came on suddenly, as it had now. A horse could develop it in a number of ways—eating too much rich grass, having toxins in the bloodstream (for whatever reason), or, as in Barbaro's case, putting too much weight on one limb. Since his injury, Barbaro had been heavily favoring his healthy back leg, causing uneven blood circulation.

But whatever the cause, the effect was always the same— the tissues joining the coffin bone to the outer wall of the hoof became inflamed, causing terrible pain. (The tissues are called laminae, hence the name of the disease.) Most of the time, the only option was to cut off the inflamed part of the hoof and try to regrow it, but some horses were in too much pain to go through that and had to be put down.

I had learned about the disease as a boy in Peru, where horsemen gave me a few coins to spend all day riding around on a horse with laminitis, hopefully stimulating blood circulation to the hoof and making the tissue grow back faster.

But few of those horses survived.

Michael told me Dr. Richardson had made his diagnosis and immediately brought together the Jacksons and Michael to discuss what should be done. There was talk of putting Barbaro down on the spot, but Michael said he felt the horse, having come this far, deserved every chance to live—as long as he wasn't in pain. Dr. Richardson agreed, saying he thought he could control the pain and give Barbaro an opportunity to fight the odds.

When he announced the news to the press, Dr. Richardson wasn't the least bit optimistic. The bones Barbaro fractured in the Preakness were healing, he said, "but the left hind foot is basically as bad a laminitis as you can have." He had cut off 80 percent of the hoof and hoped it would grow back, but "that's like regrowing a nail in humans after it's been pulled out," he said. "Horses do recover, but it's a long shot. I'm not going to sugarcoat the situation. It is a poor percentage for recovery, but as long as he's not suffering, we will continue to try."

Sitting at home in New York, I closed my eyes and ran my hands through my hair. This was disastrous news. Barbaro now had two foes to beat, a shattered leg and a terrible disease, and he had to beat them both if he was going to survive and have the decent life we had all imagined for him.

I had to get to New Bolton to see him. I hadn't been back in a month, since my visit shortly after the Belmont. My heart and prayers were with him, but I had been struggling to find the free time I needed. As always, I was busy. I had traveled to California and Canada to ride in stakes races, and

I also went to Peru because it had been six months since my mother's death and my family held a commemoration. I had been going here, there, and everywhere except New Bolton.

Strictly by coincidence, Liliana stopped by the clinic on the day Dr. Richardson announced Barbaro had laminitis. She had driven to Philadelphia to pick up Patty and Louis, who were spending a few days with my brother Anibal's family, and she decided on her own to go see Barbaro, since she was nearby. She didn't know about the bad news, but she figured it out. The Barbaro she saw that morning wasn't anything like the Barbaro we had seen in June. He wouldn't take any fruit and candy she offered, and in fact, wouldn't even look at her when she called his name. He just stared out the windows.

Liliana finally left after twenty minutes and called me on her cell phone. "You better get down here in a hurry if you want to see Barbaro. He is not doing well at all. I'm worried he might not make it," she said. Her voice was shaking.

As soon as I heard from her, I spent the rest of that afternoon—a Thursday—figuring out how I could get to New Bolton. I might be saying good-bye, so there was no time to waste.

I came up with a plan. At that time of year, Belmont turned its Friday racing card into a twilight event, with the first race going off at 3:00 p.m., two hours later than normal. I had a full card of mounts scheduled, but if I got up really early, I could get down to New Bolton, see Barbaro, and get back in time for the first race. Those extra two hours opened the window of opportunity just wide enough for me.

Liliana made it home that evening with Patty and Louis,

and when she heard my idea, volunteered to turn right back around the next morning and drive me down to New Bolton. As tired as I was from riding, she was just as tired from driving. But she was crushed about Barbaro and wanted to go back and see him.

We arranged for people to stay with the kids and got up at 4:00 a.m. the next day. The roads were empty, and Liliana made great time; we were at New Bolton shortly after sunrise. There had been a ton of press around the day before for Dr. Richardson's announcement about laminitis, but the place was empty and quiet now. Liliana and I walked in, said hello to the staff, put on scrubs, and went to see Barbaro.

I called out to Barbaro when I stepped into his stall, as I had at the start of each of my previous visits.

"Hey, Barbaro. Hey, fella," I said.

He wouldn't look at me. He had been staring out the windows before I came in, and he didn't move. I knew he had heard me. He was simply ignoring me.

"Look here, boy," I said. "I got apples. I got carrots and candy."

Normally, he rushed to greet me, knowing what I had. But this time, he just stared. His silence and stillness gave me chills.

"What's up, boy?" I said softly. "What's the matter? Don't you want something to eat?"

I walked across the room and got in between him and the window, inserting myself into his view like a child wanting attention. He turned from the window and gave me an annoyed look; had he been human he would have said, "Leave me alone, OK?"

If you looked at him, you could understand why he was down. There were fiberglass casts on both of his back legs now, one protecting the broken leg and the other for his laminitis. He was hooked up to a maze of medicine drips and monitors; Dr. Richardson had said he would be on a lot of pain medication. But maybe worst of all, from Barbaro's perspective, he was stuck inside.

Barbaro loved the grass, the outdoors, running, his training routine. He even loved watching other horses run. He bloomed when he was outside, literally almost swelling up with enthusiasm. But at New Bolton he had been stuck in this room for weeks, his condition too delicate for a trip outside, where he could take a bad step or get an infection.

As down as he was about being in pain, I think he was mostly depressed because he felt like a captive.

I held out a baby carrot, his favorite snack. He took it but spit it on the ground.

"Come on, boy," I purred. "This makes you happy."

I held out a red apple, which he usually swallowed whole. He knocked it out of my hand with his nose.

I stared at him. He stared out the window.

"I guess you don't want any company, huh?" I asked.

I walked across the straw floor and out the door, and spoke to one of the nurses.

"Boy, he's not himself," I said.

She nodded. Every person at the clinic had learned that Barbaro would always tell if he was happy or sad, or whether he had slept well. I had never known a horse that could convey his feelings so clearly.

He obviously was in no mood for company, so I went back to the kitchen to get a cup of coffee. I had visited enough that the staff knew me. I sat in the kitchen and talked to them, and then went out to the front desk to talk to the vets and admissions people. I looked over the latest rounds of flowers, get-well cards, and stuffed animals that had arrived; they took up an entire hallway, and many more surely would be coming now, since it had been announced Barbaro had laminitis.

After an hour I decided to give the horse another try. I walked over to the ICU, put scrubs back on, and crept into his room. When I said his name, he turned from the window to look at me and pricked his ears. He seemed happier.

"Hey, boy," I said, walking to him. "You're feeling better now?"

When I offered him a carrot, he took it and gulped it. "That's my guy," I said. He let me pat him and play with his ears, a reminder of the better times we had shared. I had always played with his ears when we were in a post parade.

Soon, he put his head on my shoulder, as he had that night at Pimlico, and I stroked his great muscular neck over and over. After a few minutes, I realized he had fallen asleep. He awoke soon enough, but I spent another hour with him, talking to him, and walking him around the room gently and slowly.

Then, suddenly, like a thunderstorm blowing in, his mood changed again, and he was quite clearly finished with the visit. He left me and turned back to his window. I felt like I was in a business meeting with an executive who was suddenly ready for his next appointment. He had had enough.

The rejection didn't hurt my feelings so much as make me

sad. He was not the same horse that had breezed through his first weeks after surgery.

Liliana and I left and drove back to New York for the twilight racing card at Belmont. I was badly shaken by what I had seen. Barbaro had always been so upbeat and feisty. He had made it easy for you to feel good about him and confident about his recovery.

But this time, he was obviously down—very down. I was sad as we drove toward New York. I wondered what was going on in his head. Was he in pain? Was he afraid? Did he want to be training and racing? What was he thinking? He had offered no clues, which was so unlike him. He was just still and silent. That was hard to watch. He showed no emotion at all. It gave me the chills to think about it. If he had made some noise or rolled around or done anything, at least he would have shown some sign of life. But he was as quiet as the sunrise Liliana and I had seen earlier that day.

I prayed it wasn't the last time I would see him, but I wondered how much he could take before he gave in. Between a shattered leg, laminitis, and being stuck inside for weeks on end, he was going through a lot.

When I got to Belmont, I told a couple of friends where I had been, and soon enough, reporters wanted to talk to me. I gave them my impressions of Barbaro's condition, saying that he seemed in better shape than I had expected for a horse with laminitis, but that he was, undoubtedly, in a fight for his life.

"All we can do now is hope and pray," I said. "We're going to need a miracle."

CHAPTER 14

An Inspiring Comeback

Every year from late July to early September, many of America's best horses, jockeys, and trainers battle it out for six weeks at the Saratoga Race Course in upstate New York, in front of stands packed with racing fans. Since 1999, when I made my first visit to the track nicknamed "the Spa," I had become a regular rider there. In 2002 I won fifty-four races to take the riding title, beating out Jerry Bailey, who had won the title for four years in a row until I bested him. In 2004 I won the meet's biggest race, the Travers Stakes, on Birdstone. In 2005 I won the riding title again.

In 2006, the summer of Barbaro, I had another strong meet, winning the Saratoga Special and forty-five other races to capture my third riding title in five years. But that summer was unlike any other. No matter which horses I rode or how many races I won, I was, to most fans, the jockey of just one horse—the one fighting for his life at the New Bolton Center.

Barbaro never got within three hundred miles of Saratoga, but he was such a presence at the meet, from start to finish, that it felt like he was parading up and down the track between races. Every day, fans stopped me on my way from the jockeys' room to the paddock, thanked me, and told me how sorry they were. Some said they were praying for me, and of course, for Barbaro, too. Some were backyard horsemen who had dealt with laminitis and wanted me to pass along treatment suggestions to Dr. Richardson. Others were just regular folks who, like me, had fallen in love with Barbaro and had their hearts broken by his injury. I could barely get on and off a horse without Barbaro coming up.

Before the grim announcement that Barbaro had laminitis, I thought legions of people were rooting for him mostly because they had been watching on TV when he won the Kentucky Derby and broke down two weeks later, and they couldn't help feeling sad for this incredible horse. But after the news broke about his laminitis a few days before the Saratoga meet, he staged a more dramatic rally than any he ever pulled on a racetrack. Surviving laminitis was a crazy long shot, but he pulled it off, beating back a disease that often proved fatal. And suddenly, people felt more than just sympathy; they were inspired by his courage and his will to live.

I know I was. When I left the New Bolton Center that day in July, I doubted I would see him again. I had seen too many horses die from laminitis. But in the immediate days after the onset of the disease, Barbaro seemed to maintain a positive outlook, eating well, sleeping soundly, and bearing whatever pain he was feeling with grace and strength. He spent several hours a day in a sling to control his movements. The first days were critical, and instead of getting worse, Barbaro got better.

After several weeks, Dr. Richardson announced in early August that the hoof that had been cut off was starting to grow back, and also, the broken leg was healing. In fact, the only reason the broken leg was still in a cast, as opposed to a bandage, was because it needed extra support since it was compensating for the leg with laminitis and bearing most of Barbaro's weight.

Barbaro progressed so rapidly that by mid-August Dr. Richardson decided he could go outside for the first time since he had been admitted. After nearly three months in the ICU, he began making daily fifteen-minute outings to a grassy area nearby. He was able to graze, enjoy the fresh air, be a horse again. This was an enormous step in the right direction. I knew the sunshine would boost his spirits.

Dr. Richardson continued to deliver good news as the Saratoga meet progressed. On August 17 he told the press that Barbaro had been taken off pain medication and no longer needed to spend time in a sling. Two days later, the doctor reported that the hoof that had been stricken with laminitis was improved to the point that it needed just a bandage now instead of a cast.

If there had been any way for me to get to the New Bolton Center, I would have gone just to give Barbaro a hug. He was fighting for his life with the same ferocity he had shown on the track. He knew he was injured and sick, but he wanted to live.

I think, in the end, his will to survive became the backbone of his popularity. The worst imaginable obstacles had been thrown in his path, but he refused to give in. People could find inspiration in that. We all go through bad times, but here this horse was showing us that it was possible to keep going, that anything could be overcome. Barbaro was showing us courage.

I noticed a change in my Barbaro mail, piles of which I was continuing to receive even though it had been months since Barbaro's breakdown and even longer since our Kentucky Derby victory. Instead of just expressing their sympathy and well wishes, people began telling me their stories. A man in Georgia, suffering from stomach cancer, wrote that he had been depressed about his chances of overcoming his illness, but after seeing Barbaro fight so hard, had recommitted himself to beating the odds. Barbaro had changed his life, he said. The letter moved me beyond words, and I sat down and wrote right back, saying I would be praying for him.

I received a similar letter from a man with bipolar disorder, a devastating mental illness. He wrote that he was learning from Barbaro not to give in to bad news; that he knew now more than ever how important it is to stay positive because anything is possible. When I mentioned the letter to Michael during one of our phone calls, he said he had received one from a youngster in Africa who was battling AIDS and had found Barbaro's courage inspiring.

Meanwhile, the news from the New Bolton Center only got better and better. Dr. Richardson said the cast on the broken leg could come off soon; the bones had almost healed,

and the joints had fused. Barbaro "needs to continue to improve over the next few months before we will have a better
idea about his long term comfort," the doctor told the press,
"but his appetite and his attitude right now are phenomenal;
he attacks his feed, and when he goes out to graze, acts like he
thinks he could train. Right now, he is a surprisingly happy
horse. He is gaining weight and has had his pain medications
reduced without any effect on his well-being. His strength
and overall appearance have been improving since he became
well enough to be walked outside."

I left Saratoga immediately after the last race on Labor
Day, the final day of the six-week meet, and drove back to my
house near Belmont Park, arriving at 9:00 p.m. Seven hours
later, at 4:00 a.m., I was out of the house and on my way to the
New Bolton Center with Liliana and Louis. It was a miracle,
I told Liliana, that we were coming to see him again after that
awful visit in July.

At the clinic, we greeted the people working the front
desk, walked back to the ICU, put on scrubs, and went in to
see Barbaro. He was looking out his window, but when he
heard my voice, he turned and came to the front of his stall.
He was in a playful mood and looked terrific. The scar from
his surgery was starting to fade, and he had put on weight.
We fed him baby carrots, peppermints, and sugar cubes from
his basket. He took them with big gulps. We stayed for an
hour, and as I left, I told Ray Gonzales to take care of him
while I was gone. Ray grinned and said he would.

Two weeks later, Liliana and I decided one night to get up
early the next day and go see Barbaro again. It was a day off

at Belmont, so I didn't have anything going. We were used to the routine by now, rising before dawn, Liliana driving the empty highways as the sun rose, me sleeping in the passenger seat. At the clinic, we put on our scrubs, went into the ICU, greeted him, patted him, fed his snack habit. He was continuing to put on weight, and if anything, looked better than he had two weeks earlier.

When we got ready to leave, we changed out of our scrubs and stopped by the front desk to say good-bye. Karen, one of the women who worked the desk, asked if we wanted to see Dr. Richardson. I said we didn't want to bother him; he was busy, and we were just here to see the horse. But Karen said, "Dr. Richardson isn't in surgery. Would you like to take Barbaro out to graze? Dr. Richardson might take him,"

I couldn't say yes fast enough. She called the doctor, who was somewhere on the grounds. He said he would be right over.

Either Michael or Dr. Richardson had been taking Barbaro out to graze, usually in the afternoons, when I was seldom there. But now, when Dr. Richardson came to the front desk, we shook hands and he said he would gladly change the routine so I could see Barbaro outside.

Liliana and I went back to the ICU with the doctor, put on scrubs, and went in to see Barbaro. Dr. Richardson attached a chain shank to his bridle and led him out of the stall. He seemed excited.

To get outside, Barbaro had to walk about fifty feet through the ICU and out a set of double doors. Watching him walk sent shivers down my spine. He could put weight on both of his back legs. The one that had shattered in the Preakness was crooked now, permanently bent at the hock. But Barbaro had figured out how to use it. He walked with his head high, so proud you had to smile. You could just see him thinking, "You know what? I'm going to pull this off. I'm really going to beat this."

Once he was through the double doors and in the sun, he crossed a small paved area behind the ICU building and walked up an incline to a grassy area. Dr. Richardson held the shank tightly. Barbaro lowered his head and nibbled on some grass, and then raised his head and looked around. No one could have come away thinking he was sad or depressed. He was his normal, upbeat, curious self.

A barn cat was perched on the top of the fence that surrounded Barbaro's patch of grass. Barbaro spotted him as soon as he raised his head from grazing, and his ears pricked—he wanted to play. The cat was a striped gray tabby named Felix who, like most barn cats, was used to horses and not the least bit afraid to be approached by a creature so large. Barbaro nuzzled Felix with his nose, raised his head up, then ducked and nuzzled Felix again. He was having fun.

When he tired of Felix, he put his head down to graze again. Dr. Richardson let me hold the shank. When Barbaro came up, I stroked his nose and told him I knew how happy he was to be outside. You could see it made him feel whole again. He spotted a cow in a nearby field, and his ears pricked. Then he saw a filly walking down a sidewalk across from where he stood, and that really got his attention. His eyes lit, he sniffed deeply, and he raised up on his haunches, almost reared. I looked at Dr. Richardson. We both laughed. Typical male, ogling the girls.

It was great to be with him in the sunshine. Finally, after twenty minutes, we took him back in, put him in his stall, and said our good-byes. As Liliana and I drove home, I felt better than I ever had about his chances of making it. He had been through so much, but he was really moving in the right direction.

Every day there was more and more happiness in the huge community of Barbaro fans. The toy company that made Beanie Babies, the popular plush toys, brought out a Barbaro doll, with a portion of all sales going to the Barbaro Fund. Posters on the New Bolton Center and Tim Woolley Web sites sounded increasingly hopeful, with the latter community now calling itself the "Fans of Barbaro," or FOBs for short.

The horse continued to give them all a reason to cheer. His left hoof continued to grow back and was wrapped in just a bandage instead of a cast. In early October Dr. Richardson changed the cast on the right leg, trimmed the left hoof, and put on a new shoe. Barbaro woke up in the recovery pool and grazed later that day. "There are no signs of infection, and the primary incisions have healed surprisingly well," Dr. Richardson said. It was impossible not to be optimistic.

In early November, there was another huge positive step. Dr. Richardson put Barbaro under, took off the cast on his broken leg, and replaced it with a padded bandage. Barbaro had worn a cast on that leg for more than five months, since his surgery on the day after the Preakness. The switch to a bandage was significant; he was really on his way. Barbaro woke up in the recovery pool and "walked easily back to his stall using all of his legs quite well," Dr. Richardson said. The doctor also checked the left hind hoof while Barbaro was under and said it was continuing to grow. He did sound a note of caution, saying it would still be several months before he knew how much of the foot would return.

After my visits in September, I was unable to get back to New Bolton for a little while. The Breeders' Cup was held in early November at Churchill Downs, and that took up a lot of my time and concentration. But although I couldn't be with Barbaro, I spoke to Michael and Gretchen several times for updates and followed the news online, feeling more and more confident all the while.

I went to Churchill Downs for the Breeders' Cup almost exactly six months after winning the Kentucky Derby there. It was impossible for me not to think about Barbaro. This was where his greatest triumph had come, where he had shown the world what a champion he was. It was also where he had started and finished a race for the last time. That seemed like a lifetime ago, and it was so sad to think about what the past six months had been like for him. But on the other hand, he had adjusted to a new life and was beating the challenges put before him. I was so proud of him.

As if the trip to Louisville alone wasn't emotional enough, I rode a horse for Michael in the Breeders' Cup Distaff, a dirt race for fillies and mares. The filly's name was Round Pond. She was a four-year-old that had a strong finishing kick and had won a major stakes race before being sidelined by a bone chip in her knee and related foot problems. Following her recovery, Michael had spent months getting her in shape to race.

She wasn't one of the favorites in the Distaff, leaving the starting gate as a 15–1 shot, well behind the 5–2 co-favorites, an older mare named Fleet Indian and a three-year-old named Pine Island. But the race unfolded like a dream. I settled her into a stalking position, just behind the early leader, a speedball. The favorites were behind me, and as we turned for home, I waited for a hole to open on the rail, and one did. I shot through and pulled away to win easily, by four and a half lengths.

Only later did I learn that both co-favorites had been pulled up with injuries behind me, a sad development that made me feel less joyous in victory. Pine Island, it turned out, had dislocated the fetlock joint in her left leg and was put down in her barn several hours after the race because the wound was open and likely contaminated. People couldn't believe the incredible, sad coincidence of Barbaro's trainer and jockey coming back to Churchill and winning a Breeders' Cup race that was so similar to Barbaro's tragic Preakness.

Of course, I was still thrilled to have won—this was just my third Breeders' Cup win—but I felt Barbaro's presence hovering over me. Even though Round Pond wore saddle cloth No. 2, I somehow got it into my head that she had worn No. 8, Barbaro's number in the Kentucky Derby. After the race I said to Liliana, "Isn't it an amazing coincidence that Round Pond wore No. 8, just like Barbaro?" Liliana didn't respond. I said the same thing to one of the exercise riders, how amazing it was that both horses wore No. 8. Later, back at the hotel that night, I realized my mistake. "I swear I looked at that saddle cloth and saw No. 8," I told Liliana. She looked at me like I was crazy. And maybe I was. Being back at Churchill, I was "channeling" the horse that had taken me to the Derby winner's circle.

Things slowed down for me after the Breeders' Cup and I made it back to New Bolton on a Tuesday in late November. That was the six-month anniversary of the Preakness, so I felt it was a good day to see Barbaro and mark his progress. Also, if I didn't see him then, I wasn't sure when I would. I was going to Japan for the World Racing Championships and otherwise would be based in South Florida, racing at Calder and Gulfstream, through the winter and early spring. I wouldn't be able to just slip away for a visit on a day off. I would be too far from New Bolton for that.

So on November 20 I went down with Liliana and Louis. We stopped at the front desk and said hello to the gang, then went back to the ICU. This was my sixth visit, and for the first time, Barbaro was in a different stall. His wing of the ICU was being painted, so he had been moved through a set of doors and into a larger stall in what New Bolton called its NICU—the neonatal intensive care unit. It was a lot like his old stall, with the rectangular windows he could look out, only he had a little more room to move around.

He was in a feisty mood at first, biting and snapping when I tried to pet him and feed him. The usual morning staff was working, including Ray Gonzales and Kasey McCafferty, the ICU's head nurse. They told me he had been like this all morning. I stepped away and gave him a few minutes to calm down. While I waited, I signed Kasey's Barbaro Beanie Baby and a few other items for the nurses. They had done such an incredible job. I was more than happy to meet their requests.

When I went back to Barbaro, he was in a better mood. I

looked into his eyes, petted him, spoke to him, and slipped into his stall. He was happy to see me, and as cuddly as a kitten when I hugged him. One of the nurses put a dash of molasses on my hand, and Barbaro licked it right off.

Then, to my surprise, Gretchen Jackson joined us with one of her grandchildren. Karen, the girl who worked at the front desk, had called her and told her I was here, and she came right away. As usual, she had a basket of grass from her farm, and Barbaro dug right in when she gave it to him.

After his snack, he was so relaxed he lay down for a nap, maneuvering his crooked leg as if it had been that way from birth. I got down on the floor with him, stroking him and speaking to him softly. He always responded to voices.

I got up and went back out to visit with Gretchen. She asked where I thought Barbaro should go when he was released from New Bolton. That stopped me cold. What? I didn't know that was even being considered. But Gretchen said he had come so far and his prospects were so promising that she, her husband, and Dr. Richardson had started talking about where he should live. My heart soared.

The Jacksons lived on a nice farm nearby. That was an option. Barbaro had loved being at Michael's barn at Fair Hill, but that was a public park and there were security concerns. The Jacksons also had discussed sending him to Three Chimneys Farm, the Kentucky breeding establishment where his sire, Dynaformer, lived.

I told Gretchen he certainly would enjoy the nice weather in Florida, selfishly thinking how nice it would be to have him so close to my home there. Gretchen smiled and agreed

Florida would suit him, but said she might want him a little closer than that so she could keep visiting him.

After a few minutes Gretchen got ready to leave. As she departed, Dr. Richardson had a break in his schedule and joined us. Barbaro unfolded his legs and got right up when he heard the doctor's voice, looking guilty, like a security guard who had been caught sleeping on the job. There was nothing wrong with him lying down, but he had such respect for the doctor that he instinctively stood. I told the doctor how great Barbaro looked, and how exciting it was just to be considering sending him elsewhere.

Dr. Richardson couldn't stay for long, but Liliana, Louis, and I hung around for another hour. Louis had been a little fearful at first because Barbaro was so snappy when we arrived, but the nurses took Louis around to meet some of the other "patients" in the NICU. Barbaro's next-door neighbor was an alpaca named Dobby who had a broken leg and a cast up to his hip. Louis fed and petted Dobby, met several other horses, and eventually felt comfortable enough with Barbaro to pet him.

We were in no hurry to leave, but as lunchtime approached, we had to get back to New York to get ready for the trip to Japan. I went back into Barbaro's stall to say good-bye. He was back on his feet, as he had been since Dr. Richardson arrived, and he was happy, calm, and eager for friendship. I fed him a carrot, looked in his eyes, and spoke to him.

"Be well, *mi amigo*."

Be well, my friend.

I hugged him, turned, and left, never once thinking that I had just seen him for the last time.

CHAPTER 15

A Sudden Turn for the Worse

On a sunny weekday morning in South Florida in the last week of December, I got up early and went to the gym to run on the treadmill. When I got home, Liliana was upset, tearful, almost inconsolable.

"What's wrong?" I asked, putting my arm around her.

Between sobs she told me CNN had broadcast something about Barbaro's having suffered a setback. The network was cycling through the same news broadcast every hour, so I waited to see what she had seen.

I wasn't that concerned. Many times in the past eight months things had looked bad for Barbaro for one reason or another—the onset of laminitis, another cast change, another surgery—but Barbaro had always pulled through. How bad could this be? I would have heard if there was a real problem.

Besides, when I had last seen him at New Bolton just before Thanksgiving, he looked so healthy that it was hard to imagine anything going wrong. He was moving with ease, eating well, looking at the world through shining eyes. True, the doctor had warned that he wasn't completely out of the woods and wouldn't be for some time, but having seen the horse, I wasn't nearly as worried as I had been in, say, July, when he first came down with laminitis.

I tried to make Liliana feel better as I waited for the CNN report. I thought maybe she had just seen a year-in-review segment detailing the ups and downs Barbaro had experienced in 2006, showing video of him when he wasn't doing well. I was sure everything would be fine.

But then the report came on, and the bottom fell out of my stomach.

It wasn't a year-in-review broadcast. It was new video taken of Barbaro walking out of his stall at New Bolton. He didn't look like the same horse I had seen six weeks earlier. He had lost weight to the point that he was skinny, startlingly so. His coat had lost its sparkle and now looked washed out. He walked with his head slung low, like he was depressed, struggling just to put one foot in front of the other. And he was limping badly on his crooked leg.

"What's wrong with him, Edgar?" Liliana cried.

I had to admit, I didn't have a clue. Even when he had casts on both of his hind legs, he had come out of his stall with an attitude, showing off his pride. It was stunning to see him limping slowly with his head down and the spirit gone from his eyes, like a candle that had been blown out. Worst of all, his broken leg was dragging. It was clear now that it had healed at an odd angle, curving underneath his body, no doubt because he had been forced to keep his weight on it rather than the foot with laminitis.

I listened to what was being reported and was depressed to learn that there had been what Dr. Richardson called a "significant" setback, primarily due to laminitis. Five months after the disease had appeared in the left hind foot, it was still very much in play. A cast had been put back on because the hoof was not growing back on the inner side and the foot was unstable. Dr. Richardson had gone in to remove more damaged tissue.

Barbaro was back on a heavy course of pain medication. His chances of beating laminitis really were no better than they had been back in July, when things looked so bleak.

I snapped off the television. I didn't want to see that awful video again.

What in the world had happened? I hadn't spoken to Michael or Gretchen since mid-December and was upset to be so out of the loop.

I called Michael, who was at Palm Meadows working his horses, having returned to Florida for the winter racing season. He filled me in. After months of positive news, the ICU nurses began noticing changes in Barbaro around Christmas. He was favoring the foot with laminitis when he went out to graze. He became more agitated, didn't settle as easily, and lost some of his appetite. A foot specialist from Kentucky was brought in, and his evaluation was grim. The foot wasn't getting any better, and neither were Barbaro's chances of beating laminitis.

"Michael, he doesn't look good at all," I said on the phone. "I hated what I saw on TV this morning."

Michael agreed.

"I don't know. I think he is trying to tell us something, Michael," I said. "He has fought for eight months. He has overcome so much. But when I see him limping out of his stall with his head down, I think he is telling us he is hurting. I think he is telling us he is in pain.

"Michael, he might be telling us that he has fought long enough."

Michael said he would be heading up to Pennsylvania in early January to celebrate his mother's birthday, and planned to go to New Bolton to see the horse. He promised to give me an update.

Two weeks later, I rode a horse for Michael at Gulfstream. Usually, when I got on one of Michael's horses, we discussed only the upcoming race in the paddock, but this time, we talked about Barbaro. He had, in fact, seen the horse, and the news wasn't good. Barbaro had been lying down in his stall and didn't even get up to greet Michael. He was tired of dealing with that crooked leg. He just raised his head. Michael was horrified at how far he had slipped. He had shrunken, lost a ton of weight.

After our conversation, I rode Michael's horse, got off, showered, changed, and got ready for the next race—that's what I do. But deep inside, I just wanted to go to New Bolton and give Barbaro a treat out of his basket. Or get down on the floor with him as he rested. Or take him out to graze.

I thought about the man with cancer who had written me, saying he was rededicating himself to beating his disease because he had seen Barbaro fighting so hard. What would this news do to him? And what would it do to the man with bi-polar disorder who also had found inspiration in Barbaro's determination?

I thought about all those people who had sent me cards, letters, hats, poems, and T-shirts—people who had never touched Barbaro, but loved him. What would they think? How would they feel?

Mostly, I thought about Barbaro. He was suffering now. No one had to tell me. I knew it from eleven hundred miles away. He had been through more surgeries than any human could handle, laminitis, pain, drugs, the tedium of being stuck inside for months—and he had fought it all. I feared now that he had nothing left to give.

I followed his condition on the Internet for the next few days. The Jacksons and Dr. Richardson wanted to keep trying to save him. He had come so far and showed such courage that it seemed possible he could do anything. I had to agree. And sure enough, in the next couple days he stabilized. He was spending a few hours a day in the sling. His laminitis wasn't worsening.

Toward the end of January I went to Peru for a memorial service marking the first anniversary of my mother's death. My whole family gathered. The year had been an unforget-table, emotional time for me, and my mother had never been far from my thoughts. Being around people who felt the same way gave me comfort.

The trip coincided with the 2007 Eclipse Awards Dinner in California. The Eclipses are the equivalent of the Oscars for horse racing, the highest honor you can receive. Every year, voters pick the top horses in all categories (two-year-old filly, three-year-old colt, and so on) and also the top owner, trainer, and jockey. I had been nominated four times and gone to the dinners, but I had never won. This time, I couldn't go because I was in Peru, and honestly, I didn't think I would win anyway. I had won the Kentucky Derby, the Breeders' Cup Distaff, and 246 other races in 2006, and my horses had won almost $20 million in earnings, but another jockey, Garrett Gomez, had garnered more stakes wins and earnings than anyone.

Late on the night of the dinner, while I was driving my brother Anibal to the Lima airport for his flight back to Philadelphia, I received a call from a friend—I had won the Eclipse Award!

It was a thrill, to say the least. I was in the car with several of my brothers and sisters, and they all cheered and hugged me. By the time I got home from the airport, the word had spread, our house had filled with friends, and the celebration was under way. It lasted well into the night.

I was deeply honored to be recognized as the best in my field, but I felt I had won strictly because of Barbaro. The public had fallen in love with him. A vote for me was a vote for him, and people wanted to support him. I credited him 100 percent with my victory. He was the superstar.

When I got back to Florida a day later, I called Michael. Again, the news was relatively good. Dr. Richardson had put Barbaro under, changed the cast on his left foot, and put a cast back on his right foot for additional support. Barbaro was eating well and taking a little less pain medication.

Maybe it had all just been a temporary setback, a scare. Maybe he was going to overcome again.

On Thursday, January 25, Dr. Richardson put him under, changed the cast on his left hind foot, removed the cast from his right hind foot, and put on a supportive brace. Barbaro woke up in the pool, and Dr. Richardson said he was doing well.

Then two days later, on the twenty-seventh, Michael called me. I knew the news was bad before I picked up, and indeed, there was a new complication. An abscess had developed on Barbaro's right hind foot, and while it wasn't laminitis, it was intensely painful. Dr. Richardson couldn't treat it if there was a cast on the leg, so he had elected to insert a plate and two steel pins, eliminating all weight bearing from the foot. It was a risky move because the foot could fracture, and the shift in weight raised the possibility of laminitis developing in the front feet. But Dr. Richardson saw no alternative.

When Michael called, Barbaro was out of recovery and, it seemed, doing OK. I asked Michael what the odds of him surviving were, and with deep sadness in his voice, Michael said the odds were getting slimmer. He had so much going against him.

"Why don't they just put him down?" I asked.

Michael said the Jacksons and Dr. Richardson felt that since they had come this far and given Barbaro every chance to live, they should give him this chance, too.

This last chance.

Barbaro made it through that night and the next day, seemingly stabilizing. I slept poorly, aware of the long odds he now faced. I wanted badly to go to the New Bolton Center, but I had to fly to Peru for another jockeys' championship event. A number of American-based riders were coming in, and Monterrico was expecting a big day. I was a key part of the event and felt I simply couldn't miss it.

I arrived in Lima late Sunday night, got up the next morning, and went to a reception for the jockeys at the Hilton. Before it started, an old friend and distant relative of Liliana's came up to me and said, "I'm really sorry to hear about Barbaro." A crowd started to gather around us. I thought he was saying he was sorry about the horse having broken down in the first place eight months earlier. I smiled and said, "Barbaro is getting there, my friend. He wasn't doing well, but the doctor put in a plate and two new screws, and they say he is doing better."

My friend had a terrible expression on his face. "Edgar, I'm sorry, so sorry, but they put that horse down this morning. I just heard it on the radio," he said.

I just stared at him. I was speechless. Why hadn't anyone called?

The news hit me like a punch in the face. I didn't want to show my sadness because I was there to promote a competition in front of hundreds of people, but I collapsed inside. I wanted to cry. I would rather have been anywhere else. I would rather have been at the New Bolton Center. I wished someone had let me know he was going to be put down. I would have come from Florida. I would have come from Peru. With a little advance notice, I would have come from anywhere just to hold Barbaro one last time. But I was out of the country, and with the emotion of the moment overwhelming everyone, there had been a breakdown in communication.

As it was, I had to go into the press conference in Lima. I stumbled through the motions, but then the American media found me—CNN, NBC, ESPN, and more—and I went to a TV studio and did satellite interviews for hours. "How do you feel?" they asked repeatedly. I told them I didn't have the words to express my sadness. Barbaro had been as intelligent and charismatic as any horse I had ever known, and he was one of the best racehorses any of us would ever see. But his career had been cut short, and now, after showing the world how to fight a tough opponent, he had lost his life. I could barely get the words out.

From there, I did a round of interviews with the media in Peru—Barbaro was a big story there because of me—and finally, there were no questions. I escaped. I needed to be alone. Tears flooded my eyes. Barbaro had done so much for me—for all of us, really. I had never seen an animal show more heart. He deserved better. He deserved to live longer.

Needless to say, I didn't feel like riding at Monterrico the next day. I was sad, so very sad, and I stumbled through the afternoon in a daze. That night, I got on a plane and flew back to Florida in time to go back to work at Gulfstream. Liliana and the kids met me as I walked in the door. Their eyes were red from crying. We hugged and wept.

In the coming days I was bombarded as never before with cards and letters. It seemed as if everyone who had written me about Barbaro felt the need to write back. Every day a new stack arrived at Gulfstream along with another at home. I carved out time to read as many as possible, usually at night, when I could be alone in a quiet house after a long day at the track.

Dear Mr. Prado,

We all grieve with you at the passing of Barbaro. How fortunate you were to play a role in his short life. You and Barbaro will forever be linked as champions.

Without your heroic efforts at the Preakness, Barbaro would not have had the chance to show his true courage, spirit, and will to survive. I thank you for giving us all the opportunity to follow him a bit longer. We are heartbroken along with you.

—*Wilmington, North Carolina*

Dear Edgar,

There is nothing right now that anyone can say to you to ease your sadness. But I wanted to thank you for loving Barbaro so much—not just because he could run, but because he was a special horse, period. You were blessed to have had the experience you had with him— and we were blessed to watch you experience it.

Thank you for continuing to visit him at the New Bolton Center after his injuries. I know it meant a lot to him—he seemed to adore you as much as you adored him. Thank God there are people in the world who love horses no matter if their legs work or not!

—*Indian Harbor Beach, Florida*

Dear Edgar,

Thank you so much for the loving attention you gave America's Barbaro. Our sympathies to you on your loss of this hero. Your mother would be proud of you and we're sure she is watching. We all love you and will follow your great career.

—*Attleboro, Massachusetts*

Dear Mr. Prado,

You gave Barbaro the opportunity to overcome his accident. The sad outcome was due solely to laminitis. Many are praying for you and lighting candles in hopes that you will find comfort and peace. May God bless you and keep you always.

—*Pittsburgh, Pennsylvania*

Dear Mr. Prado,

I wanted to write you to offer my sincere condolences for the loss of Barbaro. Please know that I have you in my heart and many prayers.

I placed a special photo of you and Barbaro in my keepsake album. I also wanted to express to you, Edgar, that I also remember your mother in many prayers, God bless her.

May you find comfort in your many memories. I'm certain Barbaro will always be with you. You were his friend.

—*Dallastown, Pennsylvania*

Ordinarily I would have found the intensity of the letters remarkable, but after hearing from Barbaro's fans for eight and a half months, I expected no less. These people loved that horse with as much genuine feeling as I did. It was humbling to have them extend the same compassion to me. What had I done? I got on Barbaro and let him take me to the winner's circle. I pulled him up when he got hurt. I made hospital visits. I just did what came naturally. I was simply along for the ride.

CHAPTER 16

"Grief Is the Price We Pay for Love"

When I was back in the States, I called around to find out exactly what had happened. I learned that Barbaro had developed laminitis in both front feet, and that at the end he was in pain and agitated, no longer the horse we had loved. He tried to bite Ray Gonzales, his close friend, when Ray fed him a baby carrot. He flicked his head oddly and refused to lie down. His eyes fell dark. He was giving in.

On that last Monday, Gretchen had called Michael in Florida at dawn, told him the time had come, and asked if he wanted to come up to be with Barbaro at the end. She broke down as she spoke. Michael said she should do what was best for the horse—don't wait, in other words. Michael heard the news on the radio later than morning.

At the end, around 10:30 a.m., the Jacksons and Dr. Richardson were with Barbaro. Gretchen brought in a last basket of grass, which he ate. She was crying, Roy was crying, everyone was crying. They put Barbaro in his sling and gave him a tranquilizer. Then they gave him a solution of barbiturates. Within a minute, he slumped in the sling. He was gone.

"We just reached a point where it was going to be difficult for him to go on without pain," Roy Jackson said at a press conference that afternoon. "It was the right decision, the right thing to do. We said all along that if it ever became too difficult for Barbaro, it would be time."

It was hard to believe he was gone. Dark red roses lay on the table in front of the Jacksons and Dr. Richardson as they spoke to reporters. Many New Bolton staffers stood in the back of the room, eyes red. By that night, the clinic was overrun with flowers sent by grieving fans.

"At a moment like this, grief is the price we pay for love," Gretchen said.

Putting Barbaro down was, indeed, the right thing to do, but we all lost something with his death. I lost a friend, my perfect teammate. The Jacksons lost a wonderful horse. Horse racing lost a star that, I believe, would have made history. And the breed lost his bloodline. How great would it have been to see Barbaro's sons and daughters race? That might have made up for some of the sadness.

But at least he was no longer suffering. That was the good news, what little there was. From the moment I had seen him on CNN in late December, I knew he was in pain. He had reached the end of what he was capable of giving, had fought so hard for so long that he finally had nothing left.

The Jacksons gave him every chance to make it. Critics have accused them of being selfish and greedy, of making Barbaro suffer just because they wanted him to become a stallion and make millions off him. I said it then and I'll say it now: These accusations are ridiculous. Barbaro was heavily insured, as most top racehorses are, and as Gretchen pointed out, the easiest thing for them to do, financially, would have been to put him down at the Preakness and just collect the insurance money. When the Jacksons decided to try to save him that day at Pimlico, less than an hour after the Preakness, they didn't even know if he was fertile. They did everything they could to save Barbaro's life for no reason other than their desire to give something back to a creature who had given them such joy. They did it out of the kindness of their hearts, because they loved him.

As for me, I'm glad I rode him. I'm glad I was part of his team, and that we became friends. He was a once-in-a-lifetime teammate. I like to watch the Derby on tape now and then, just to remember how awesome he was. I'm so glad I knew his face. I'm so glad I saw his good days—and his bad days, too. I believe God sent him down to try to show us something. He was a wonderful example of courage and grace.

I'm not sure I'll ever understand why the nation became so captivated by him. An Associated Press writer put it well in an obituary the day after Barbaro died: "So many people felt a stake in Barbaro's recovery. They imagined his pain, grimaced each time he faltered, took heart as each day passed and he was still alive, making painfully slow progress. His fight for survival was their fight, a symbol of strength, courage, and comfort—and more than anything else, a source of inspiration."

The Fans of Barbaro, his most loyal supporters, had led the way. They came together in support of the horse, posting tens of thousands of online messages. For the longest time, like so many people, they had believed he would pull through. His death devastated them. But they were determined to keep his memory alive. Nine weeks later, a Pennsylvania florist's truck pulled up to the Jacksons' farm and delivered almost two hundred Easter baskets, all sent in commemoration of Barbaro by FOBs.

A few weeks after that—on April 29, what would have been Barbaro's fourth birthday—the FOBs held what they called a "Vigil of Remembrance" during a racing day at Delaware Park. The organizers originally expected 100 people, and more than 600 came. The crowed filled a tent at the track, with many of the people wearing the Jacksons' blue-and-green colors.

The Jacksons came, and were greeted with a roar. The FOBs presented them with homemade Barbaro blankets, hats, and shirts. The FOBs had invited me also, and I desperately wanted to be there, but I was riding at Aqueduct and simply could not get out of my commitments. To make up for my absence, I sat down ahead of time, wrote out some thoughts, and e-mailed them to Jeannine Edwards, the ESPN racing commentator. I had known her since the days when I was riding in Maryland, and she did TV work for the tracks there. She was hosting the Delaware Park event and agreed to read aloud my letter, in which I thanked the fans, the Jacksons, and most of all, Barbaro, for giving me the ride of my life.

Jeannine told me later that she choked back tears as she read my words to the crowd, and that everyone in the tent, including the Jacksons, cried with her. The *Baltimore Sun* reported that "the day's most moving tribute came from someone who wasn't even there." That was me.

When I turned forty in June, the FOBs sent me a cake, cards, and presents at Belmont. (They did the same for Michael, Dr. Richardson, and the Jacksons that year.) The nicest gift, by far, was a generous $2,500 donation to one of my favorite charities—Anna House, a preschool on Belmont's backstretch for the children of the exercise riders and stable help.

The Anna House donation was an example of how fans of Barbaro channeled their passion for the horse into meaningful acts of kindness and goodness. When Barbaro was still alive, the FOBs had started rescuing retired racehorses in danger of being put to death at foreign-owned slaughterhouses operating in the United States. They found homes for the horses, sometimes at their own farms, and within a year of Barbaro's breakdown in the Preakness, had rescued almost six hundred. Instead of posting online messages about Barbaro, they posted messages about saving other horses in Barbaro's name.

They also became anti-slaughter activists. Incredibly, more than 90,000 horses had been slaughtered in 2005 for human consumption overseas. The Jacksons, like many horse lovers, were appalled, and they had used the platform of Barbaro's popularity to shed light on this disgraceful practice and stir political opposition. The FOBs picked up the scent. They had organized as a support group, but going forward, they would be front-line soldiers in the battle to see that horses were treated with more respect.

In some ways I was almost afraid when the 2007 Triple Crown season rolled around. I knew people would be talking about Barbaro, and memories—good and bad—would be stirred. He hadn't been gone long, so it wasn't an easy subject for me. I knew he was still on my mind when I awoke one night that spring after seeing him in a dream standing beside my mother under a tall shining archway. I thought: What is the message here? Why were they together? The questions had no answers, like so many of those raised during Barbaro's journey.

Like the FOBs, I decided to turn my emotion into positive action for others. I had been thinking about how to raise money for my favorite charity, the Permanently Disabled Jockeys Fund, which supports jockeys who are severely injured on the job and need help. (Whenever I get paid for an appearance or an autograph session, I give the money to that fund.) I decided to auction off the saddle Barbaro had worn during our victorious Derby. It was my favorite saddle, with a rich history—I had also used it to win two Belmonts—but there was so much interest in Barbaro that I knew it would fetch a nice price. The time was right. I could always find another saddle.

The auction was held on Derby Eve in Louisville at the annual Mint Jubilee Gala. Before I went, I called the Jacksons and told them Barbaro's saddle was being put up for auction.

"Ooh, I'd love to have that," Gretchen said.

"Well, it will be available," I replied.

"I will win that auction," she declared.

"I will get you a front-row seat," I said.

The Jacksons ended up buying the saddle for $225,000, more than I had ever hoped to raise.

I used a new Derby saddle in the race the next day, hoping it would bring me renewed luck. My mount was a nice colt named Scat Daddy that, like Barbaro, had won the Florida Derby. He wasn't undefeated, but he had won three Grade I stakes and went off at 7–1 odds. Unfortunately, he ran his worst race ever in the Derby. We were in the middle of the pack for a while, but he had nothing left at the end and finished ahead of just two of the other nineteen horses. It was disappointing.

Two weeks later, I went back to Baltimore for the Preakness. The media was all over me, asking me to go back over Barbaro's breakdown. I obliged their requests while also saying that, for the sake of my mental health, it was time to move on. Barbaro would always be in my thoughts, but I had races to run, a career to pursue.

My Preakness mount was a 25–1 shot named C P West. My mind drifted back to a year earlier as I was being loaded into the starting gate. I thought about Barbaro breaking through too soon, and about the moment when I knew I had to pull him up—what a nightmare.

This time, the race unfolded quietly. C P West ran fourth after challenging for the lead at the head of the stretch—a good performance for a colt that wasn't quite as gifted as the favorites.

To be honest, the race that I really wanted to win that day was the Barbaro Stakes, one of the races on the undercard. The Maryland Jockey Club, which runs Pimlico, had taken the Sir Barton Stakes—a Preakness-day event named after the first Triple Crown winner—and renamed it in honor of Barbaro. The Jacksons were on hand to present the trophy. I knew the big crowd would go crazy seeing us together in the winner's circle again, and I felt it would be a nice way to conclude what had been an emotionally tough year for everyone on the Barbaro "team."

My horse ran second, but I was happy anyway because Michael won the race with a horse named Chelokee. Michael's eyes welled up as the Jacksons gave him the trophy. It was a wonderful moment after all they had been through together.

In July there was another Barbaro Stakes, this time at Delaware Park. Hundreds of FOBs were on hand, and I heard my name being called during the post parade. When I looked up, I saw an entire stand of people dressed in green and blue, the Jacksons' colors. This was a race I really wanted to win.

I was on a colt named Xchanger that had set the early pace in the Preakness a few months earlier before fading badly. I kept him off the pace this time and waited for a hole to open on the rail as we turned for home. Sure enough, one appeared and we zipped through to win.

Again, the Jacksons were there to present the trophy. We shared a smile.

"Well, here we are again," Gretchen said, hugging me.

That summer Gretchen told me a psychic from England had contacted her—a well-known female psychic the police used to help solve crimes. She had phoned Gretchen out of nowhere to tell her that when Barbaro broke through the gate before the Preakness, he knew something bad was going to happen. He didn't know exactly what, the psychic said, but he was trying to send us a message that we were unable to read. In some ways, I believe this is true.

It took me a long time to come around to the idea that what happened to Barbaro, in the end, might have been a positive development. He lost his life, the world lost the chance to see his talent in full bloom, and the sport lost its strongest

Triple Crown candidate in years, but so many good things have happened because of him that, indeed, perhaps the good does outweigh the bad.

Much of the response has involved funding research into laminitis. It is a mysterious ailment, and as Barbaro's case showed, there is still a lot about it we don't know. The Jacksons have set out to lead the fight against it. They gave $3 million to the University of Pennsylvania veterinary school, in Dr. Richardson's name, to fund research into possible cures. As well, the NTRA established the Barbaro Memorial Fund and has already raised $1.5 million for laminitis research and other equine health issues. The Grayson–Jockey Club Research Foundation has approved new laminitis studies. Interest in veterinary science in general is up after Barbaro's case put it in the headlines. Gulfstream Park, where Barbaro won two races, has started the Barbaro Foundation, a scholarship program for future vets.

The respect the Jacksons showed Barbaro and their efforts to keep him alive have inspired people in and out of racing to work harder to protect these animals who give us such joy. Some tracks have switched to synthetic racing surfaces that supposedly are safer (early results are mixed) and prompted track officials everywhere to realize the importance of making their sport as safe as possible. Barbaro's injury put us on the road to change, and hopefully, that road will be long and productive. I'm only sorry he had to pay the price.

"SUCH A SAD end to the story."

I've lost count of how many people have said those words to me in the months since Barbaro died.

But was that, in fact, the end of the story? I have my doubts.

In March 2006, around the time I was winning the Florida Derby on Barbaro, his mother, La Ville Rouge, foaled another bay colt by Barbaro's sire, Dynaformer.

It was Barbaro's younger brother. His name is Nicanor.

The Jacksons, who own La Ville Rouge and the younger brother, had found Barbaro's name on an old family painting of six foxhounds that hung on a wall in their house. Nicanor is the name of another foxhound in the painting. It is also the name of my uncle, one of my mother's brothers, who lived in Peru. We were close, and like my mother, he is gone now.

Nicanor looks like a reincarnation of his older brother, with the same white star splashed on his forehead. The people who work with him say he has the same spirit.

I have a feeling about that horse. I think he is going to be something special.

As a 2006 foal, he could start racing in 2008 and will be eligible for the Triple Crown in 2009. It looks like Michael will be training him.

I feel like I'm destined to ride Nicanor, Barbaro's brother, named after my uncle. And call me crazy, but I believe with all my heart that Nicanor is going to rewrite the Barbaro story. He is going to give it a happy ending.

Wouldn't that be something? People would cheer. They would fall down crying and laughing. It would be the greatest story ever told.

ACKNOWLEDGMENTS

I couldn't have written this book without the help of many people. Greg Sher, my friend in Maryland, put the idea in my head, and got the ball rolling. John Eisenberg, my co-author, carried me through the process and went to great lengths to get everything just right. Scott Waxman landed the deal. Kate Hamill at HarperCollins understood from the starting gate where I wanted to go with this, and helped me get to the finish line. My thanks to all of you.

Roy and Gretchen Jackson gave me the chance to ride a horse as wonderful as Barbaro, for which I'll always be grateful. Michael Matz prepared the horse magnificently for the 2006 Kentucky Derby and got me ready to come home with the greatest prize in all of horseracing. Peter Brette was convinced of Barbaro's greatness from the beginning, and his confidence was infectious. Thank you all.

Once Barbaro was injured, I received incredible support from the entire racing community. To the hundreds of fans who called and sent me cards, letters, gifts, and e-mail—you made it possible for me to get through some of the toughest days I have experienced. Thank you for your support. I will never forget what you did for me.

It took a lot of years and a lot of hard work to climb the racing ladder and get in position to ride Barbaro and win the Derby. I have only had three agents in all my years, and I salute them all—Victor Sanchez, Steve Rushing, and Bob Frieze. They and so many other people helped me, especially during the early years in Boston and Maryland, that I couldn't possibly name them all, but in particular, trainers Manny Azparua, Bob Klesaris, Vinnie Blengs, Dale Capuano, Rick Dutrow, and Bobby Frankel (and also the late Scotty Schulhofner and John Tammaro) gave me a chance, put me on their best horses, and helped me get better. Thank you all.

Most of all, I want to thank my wife, Liliana, and our kids, Edgar Jr., Patty, and Louis, for always being there, and for their love. And of course, there never would have been a book without Barbaro. He was a remarkable animal and I hope I have done him justice.